the resilient
garden

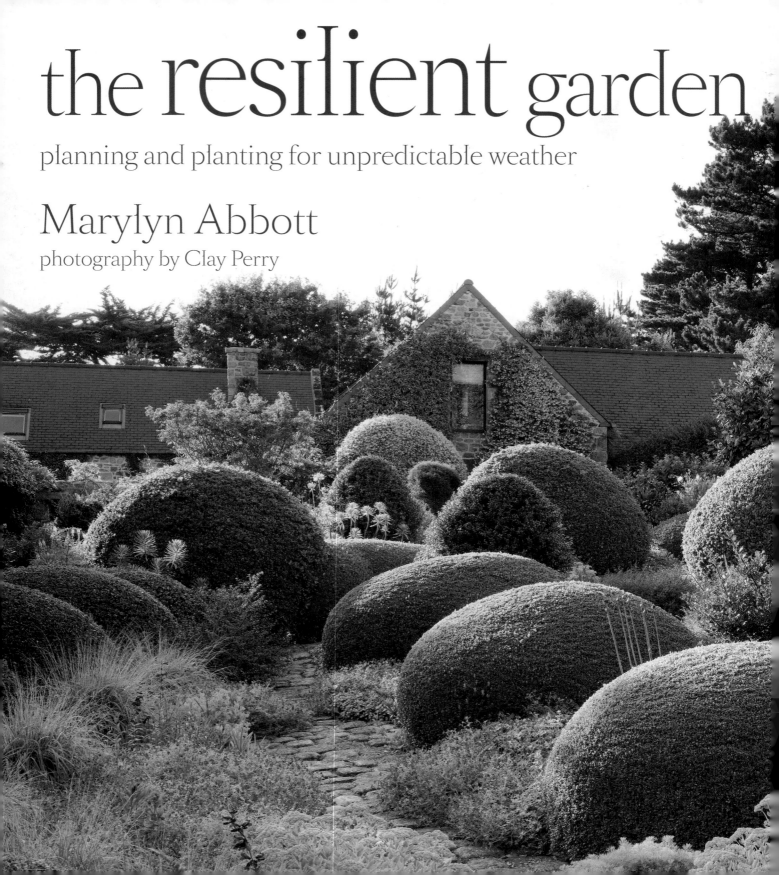

the resilient garden

planning and planting for unpredictable weather

Marylyn Abbott

photography by Clay Perry

First published in Great Britain in 2011 by
Kyle Books
23 Howland Street
London, W1T 4AY
www.kylebooks.com

ISBN: 978 1 85626 746 5

A CIP catalogue record for this title is available from the British Library

10 9 8 7 6 5 4 3 2 1

Marylyn Abbott is hereby identified as the author of this work in accordance with section 77 of the Copyright, Designs and Patents Act 1988.

Text copyright © 2011 by Marylyn Abbott
Photographs copyright © 2011 by Clay Perry *
Design copyright © 2011 by Kyle Books

Design: Geoff Hayes
Photography: Clay Perry
Project editor: Sophie Allen
Production: Sheila Smith and Nic Jones

Colour reproduction by Scanhouse
Printed in the UK by Butler Tanner & Dennis Ltd.

Marylyn's Acknowledgements
Thank you to Elwyn Swane for her sage advice on water and soil conservation and to David Glenn who introduced me years ago to dry climate perennials and still gives me never-ending advice.

Many friends travelled with me during my 'diaspora': Chris Reid who drove me through days of 40-degree heat in Eastern Australia, Carole Robert who kept me company in Spain and Italy, Rosemary Alexander in France twice and Mats Geiden von Schwarzenburg in Provence and Syria and then for arranging accommodation for me to write in Sweden during my displacement.

Thanks to the gardeners I met and who allowed me to wander through their gardens: Isabelle Vaughan at Crech Pape, Jean Schalit at Le Grand Launay, Sylvi & Patrick Quibel at Jardin du Plume, Mary Payne, friend John Coke and Jonathan Dawson for his help with the Tangier gardens.

To my editors, Charlie Ryrie and Sophie Allen for their patience and to Kyle Cathie who knows that my garden comes first and writing is for afterwards! And to Pip Heaton, who keeps West Green House administration on an even keel and never complains when I change my writing track yet again and again.

Clay Perry's Acknowledgements
I would like to thank the followimng for their help with the photography whilst working on this book. In some cases it has been impossible to include gardens for editorial reasons, but I would like to thank everyone concerned for their consideration and help: Daniel Aron, Tangier; Susan Campbell, private garden New Forest Hampshire; Jonathan Dawson for his help with the Tangier gardens; Lady Fitzwalter, Goodenstone Hall; Christopher Gibbs, Tangier; Simon Houghton, Horley Beach, Tasmania; Jonathan Jukes. Head Gardener at Marks Hall; Sir Charles & Lady Legard, Scamston Hall; Malcome & Judy Pierce, Lady Farm; Sally Razalou at the Mediterranean Garden Society's private garden, Sparoza, Greece; Sylvi & Patrick Quibel, Jardin de Plume, Normandy; Gordon Watson, Tangier; Tessa Wheeler, The Mountain, Tangier; Marco Wouters, Rancho Mimosa, Axarquia, Spain

* All images by Clay Perry except the following:

KEY: A: Alamy; APM: Allan Pollok-Morris; CN: Clive Nichols; DM: Dan Magree; GAP: GAP Photos; GC: The Garden Collection; GPL: Garden Picture Library; MM: Marianne Majerus Garden Images; PC: Pete Cassidy

Introduction: Pages 2-3 APM; 8 Matt Anker/GAP; 9 APM; 10 Clive Nichols
Protection: Pages 16-17 kind permission of Ann Howard, who owns and has renovated The Pavilion, Dangar Island; 19 left Sunniva Harte/GPL; 25 Paul Debois/GAP; 26 Jo Whitworth/GAP; 27 top left Francois De Heel/GPL; bottom left Geoff Kidd/GAP; 29 APM; 31 bottom Howard Rice/GPL; 34 left Martin Hughes-Jones/GAP, 34-35 Chris Burrows/GPL; 35 left Richard Bloom/GPL; 36 top left Georgianna Lane/GPL, top centre Harley Seaway/GPL, bottom left Marianne Majerus/MM; bottom centre Friedrich Strauss/GAP; 36-37 top right Jo Whitworth/GAP, bottom right David Burton/GPL
Water: Page 44 left Howard Rice/GPL, right Marianne Majerus/MM; 45 APM; 53 Pernilla Bergdahl/GAP; 54 Friedrich Strauss/GAP; 55 bottom left and right Juliette Wade/GPL; 56-57 GPL; 59 Michelle Garrett; 60-61 Christina Bollen/GAP; 61 bottom left Marianne Majerus/MM, bottom right Heather Edwards/GAP; 62 top Jerry Harpur/GAP, bottom Frederic Didillon/GAP; 63 left Neil Holmes/GAP, right Carol Sharp/Flowerphotos/GPL
Soil: Page 73 Howard Rice/GPL
Green Structure: Page 80 bottom right GL; 81 GL; 82-83 John Glover/GPL; 83 top Elke Borkowski/GAP, bottom Marcus Harpur/GAP; 84 APM; 85 APM; 86-87 Elke Borkowski/GAP; 87 Derek St Romaine/GC; 89 top Scottish Viewpoint/Alamy, bottom Living Landscape Trust; 90-91 Lou Metzger; 91 Martha Schwartz
Plant Groupings: Page 92 bottom DM; 93 DM; 96 left Jo Whitworth/GPL, right Mark Bolton/GPL; 97 Victoria Firmston/GAP; 98–100 DM; 101 top right, bottom left and right DM; 104 PC; 105 top left, bottom left and right PC; 106 PC
Grass Gardens: Pages 108-110 Andrew Lawson (design: Oehme & Van Sweden)/GC; 120 Ron Evans/GPL; 121 top left John Glover/GPL, right J S Sira/GPL, bottom left Sunniva Harte/GPL; 122-123 Andrew Lawson (design: Christopher Bradley-Hole, Bury Court)/GC
Seaside Gardens: Page 127 APM; 129 bottom left APM; 130 Mark Bolton/GPL; 131 top left Georgianna Lane/GPL, top right Marcus Harpur/GAP, bottom left S&O/GAP; 132 right Howard Rice/GPL; 133 left Suzie Gibbons/GPL, right Matt Anker/GAP; 134 left Andrew Lawson/GC, right Lee Avison/GAP; 135 right Howard Rice/GAP; 136-137 Clive Nichols/GAP; 139 APM
A Seaside Garden for Villa Christina: Page 140 APM; 142 left Andrew Lawson/MM, 142 bottom right Joshua McCullough/GPL; 142–143 Martin Hughes-Jones/GAP, 143 bottom left Rob Whitworth/GAP; 144 far left Jonathan Buckley/GC, left John Glover/GAP, right Nicola Stocken Tomkins/GC, far right Howard Rice/GAP; 145 APM; 146 Martin Hughes-Jones/GAP; 147 Anne Green-Armytage (design: Tony Smith)/GPL; 148 Andrew Lawson/MM; 151 Richard Bloom/GAP; 152-153 Dave Bevan/GAP; 153 Lee Avison/GAP
Plant Directory: Page 154 Dianna Jazwinski/GAP; 155 centre Richard Bloom/GAP, right John Glover/GPL; 156 left Michele Lamontagne/GPL, right John Glover/GAP; 157 bottom left Jo Whitworth/GAP, centre Dave Bevan/GAP; 158 left APM, centre Jonathan Buckley/GAP, right FhF Greenmedia/GAP; 159 centre Michael Howes/GAP, right Joshua McCullough/GPL; 160 left Geoff Kidd/GAP, centre Brigitte Thomas/GPL, right Leigh Clapp/GAP; 161 left J S Sira/GPL; 162 left Visions/GAP, right Howard Rice/GAP; 163 right Juliette Wade/GPL, left Chris Burrows/GPL; 164 top left Anne Green-Armytage/GPL, bottom left Maxine Adcock/GAP, bottom right Geoff Kidd/GAP; 165 centre Rob Whitworth/GAP; 166 top right Martin Hughes-Jones/GAP, centre Howard Rice/GAP, bottom left Dianna Jazwinski/GAP, bottom right S & O/GAP; 167 top centre Dianna Jazwinski/GAP, top right Kate Gadsby/GPL, bottom Howard Rice/GAP; 173 left Adrian Bloom/GAP; 174 right Martin Hughes-Jones/GAP; 176 centre Janet Seaton/GPL; 177 bottom left Sabina Ruber/GAP; 178 right Harley Seaway/GPL; 181 left, right and bottom centre Georgianna Lane/GPL, top centre Ron Evans/GPL; 183 bottom Marg Cousens/GAP; 185 left J S Sira/GAP, right Sunniva Harte/GPL; 186 bottom left Chris Burrows/GPL, top left Clive Nichols/GPL; 187 top centre Martin Hughes-Jones/GAP, bottom centre Neil Holmes/GAP, right FhF Greenmedia/GAP
Page 192: Image courtesy of the UK Meteorological Office

contents

I always craved a cool garden encircling an old English house…

the resilient garden

The pleasure of waking up each morning and looking across a garden to trees, fields or faraway hills has always been my ideal of the perfect life, a country life. So when I learnt that a New South Wales Government Agency had designated the land between Mittagong, the closest village, and my garden gate at Kennerton Green, as a new town I took one of the saddest decisions of my life and decided to sell my Australian garden.

My roots originally are from further south in the Mediterranean climate zone of New South Wales, Australia, where only the most resilient plants can survive; there summers may reach over 40°C (104°F), plunging into cold and frosty winters with a rainfall that seemed to diminish each year to around 58cm annually, augmented in some areas by dodgy artesian bore water, until in true Australian fashion, floods of Biblical proportions came. In the deepest recesses of my soul I always craved a cool garden encircling an old English house, the total fantasy where overgrown brambles would hide

the remains of old parterres and whimsical follies, perhaps even a swamp that had once been a lake. There would be acres of daffodils with a misting of cow parsley above bluebells and fritillaries jostling primroses in a spring meadow – every perennial that had suffered under southern New South Wales's hard blue skies would flourish in the cool northern countryside. Seventeen years ago, I found all this at West Green House in Hampshire, England, and commenced an odyssey to restore a neglected garden that still had room for the new garden concept I envisioned.

My dual existence, living between the gardens in Australia and England, ended with deep sadness with the sale of Kennerton Green in 2009 and I planned that Hampshire would for now become my home. Lodging an application for British residency produced an unexpected result, for my visa application was denied and I became instantly homeless.

Some time before, I had been asked to write about dry-climate gardens, and now with this abrupt and devastating residency refusal I was rootless, so I decided to use the time productively researching this book by visiting Europe's dry landscapes around the Mediterranean and those areas where I could go in the Middle East. My adventure began in the dry interior of Spain, travelling through to its irrigated, lush seaside resorts. In Italy I went south from Tuscany into Puglia, in Morocco from desert Marrakech across to coastal Tangier. I visited the islands of Capri and Majorca with their terraces of citrus and olive trees, and Syria. Eventually, armed with notes from earlier visits to South Africa and California and clutching my Australian passport, I arrived in the biting cold of an early spring in Sweden to borrow rooms and commence writing.

As I looked out of the Swedish window, a bright splash of the most electric hot pink caught my eye, its brilliance incongruous against the grey Nordic horizon. It was the first breaking bud on a hedge of the flowering currant *Ribes sanguineum*, obviously the most courageous of plants, for only a short time before I had admired it in a dry Murray Valley town in southern Australia. This little bud was perhaps the first sign to nudge me away from the idea of dry-climate plants and become fascinated by adaptable and resilient ones. To the currant's right was a jumble of pruned branches, which I remembered from

Above: The late winter catkins of *Corylus avellana* provide spectacle whether against snow or a cool blue Mediterranean sky.

Opposite: The catalyst plant, the flowering currant, *Ribes sanguineum*, is resilient in the widest range of climates.

Against the grey Nordic horizon… the first breaking bud on a hedge of the flowering currant Ribes sanguineum, obviously the most courageous of plants…

the previous summer as a wild planting of the species rose *Rosa glauca*. This rubrifolia rose, whose mauve-grey foliage and handsome hips are a flower arranger's delight, was obviously just as at home here as it had been in my own grandmother's outback garden in a completely contrasting climate.

Other remembered summer visions from home, bright blue lavender and *Nepeta* 'Six Hills Giant', were, I knew, imprisoned in the edges of this Stockholm garden – both stalwarts of the Mediterranean – and the spreading, fan-shaped *Cotoneaster horizontalis* was as content here as in any dry-climate rockery, alive with red berries from autumn into the midst of winter. Wheels of retrospection started as I thought of an afternoon spent with a friend and her young children at San Souci near Potsdam, Germany, exclaiming in delight at the forest floor carpeted in lily of the valley, *Convallaria majalis*, which also grew on a baking-hot bank of red soil in my New South Wales garden. That morning I had been reminded that my order of holm oaks, *Quercus ilex*, were due to be delivered in Hampshire; a tree that is always highly recommended for its tolerance of dryness was to be planted in my damp garden, so my thoughts about adaptable plants started to accelerate.

With the media describing a world climate ricocheting between intensely contrasting seasons of fire and heat and unprecedented cold and snow, with summers of catastrophic flooding or droughts decimating entire landscapes, these forgiving plants would seem to be the ones we must in future rely on. We are now all familiar with the phrases 'global warming' and 'climate change', illustrated by these climatic extremes, and the idea of the need to plant more trees to counteract our carbon footprint. We are told that energy resources are finite, and I started seriously to question whether plants happy only in specific localities had a place in plantings for the future.

Until recently, we have always considered it our right to grow what pleases us, regardless of the often excessive demands of a plant now in the wrong topography, and we have accepted the technologies that allow water to be on constant call, that every season a new enhanced plant arrives and there is a chemical to solve everything. We have not questioned our right to this bounty or whether it is desirable or sustainable, but now, as gardeners in climates subject to extreme change and contrasting conditions, surely we can no longer look at a patch of ground, dig it up, plant and expect prolific results. The desire to grow the most exotic or newly developed plants is perhaps an indulgent garden activity that cannot continue. Already the over-demand for irrigation for commercial agriculture and horticulture is creating even more dams and emptying the river systems, and a horrifying amount of artesian water is pumped to supply untenable plants, polluting fertile land in some areas with salinity, and water quality is compromised by fertilisers causing blue algae in water systems.

In utter astonishment, during my diaspora I'd witnessed in a development along Spain's southern coast a large crane lowering an ancient olive tree, gnarled and knotted from decades of harsh living, into a lawn of lush emerald green, sustained in this climate only by indecent volumes of water. This was dysfunctional gardening in practice, for I doubt very much whether the venerable olive tree could adapt from so long in a dry environment to transplantation into a lawn with water requirements that are only really sustainable in cool temperate lands. Perhaps subconsciously it was this episode, which I saw replicated in variations around the Mediteranean coast's proliferating urban developments, that first made me question the sustainability of many of the newly designed modern gardens. Perhaps these gardens are created simply as a marketing tool, built to tick the boxes for the north European second-home migrant, who yearns to soak up the sun under olive and orange trees, reclining on chaise longues placed on manicured grass.

Historically, great gardens were conceived to fulfil a patron's imagination and, if exotic plants were used, they had been gathered with immense difficulty by plant explorers and their rarity was highly appreciated. But now we can purchase and have delivered any plant we dream of, regardless of its suitability. As gardeners we must show that there can be imaginative and desirable gardens using plants that can accommodate our dreams but still tolerate many diverse growing conditions.

As a younger warm climate gardener I thought those plants described as resilient belonged only in the cactus landscape of Lanzarote, or in isolated, no-maintenance, urban planting designs, but then I realised that one of the most inspirational gardens created over two decades ago by the late Nicole de Vesion in Provence was resilient and sustainable. Her choice of plants ranged from the statuesque, deep green cyprus *Cypressus semper-virens* to multitudes of grey balls of many Mediterranean native plants that included ever-desirable lavenders, santolinas and rosemary — all prosper in both dry and colder climates. The Dutch plantsman Piet Oudolf weaves gardens of perennials and grasses together in divergent climates,

Far left: The late Nicole de Vesion's garden in Provence is an exemplar of many resilient plants.

Right: The ultra-tough cotoneaster survives all that nature can throw at it.

Historically, great gardens were conceived to fulfil a patron's imagination whilst the late Emma Keswick and Charles Jencks' landscapes consisting of just landforms and water are sublime concepts, all inspirations for designers in any climate.

It was the visions of great banks of flowers in all shades of blues to purples with lemon highlights and smudged pinks that enticed me to garden in England, but on one of the hottest days in southern Australia I saw this in reality in a display where these summer perennials in fact looked more at home than being spoilt in my English border. Nurserymen who supply plants in harsher climates have reintroduced many perennials to conditions similar to their native habitat, beautiful varieties that have become thought of as only for pampered gardens.

Gardens of predominantly green structure have come down to us from the Mediterranean's classical civilisations and this tradition was transferred in the 17th century into the embroidered parterres of the *schlösser* and *chateaux* of northern Europe. The green design was usually made from surprisingly resilient box, *Buxus* spp, a plant that continues as a mainstay in gardens from New Orleans to Oslo, along with the shiny, green, broad leaf of the Portuguese laurel, *Prunus lusitanica*, synonymous with the Victorian shrubbery, but which acted just as well to stop hot winds for me on our Australian sheep farm. All these plants are resilient with sensible care.

Plant care can go to radical levels, well illustrated in an Australian country garden I visited. Perhaps this garden was a wished-for oasis, an antidote to the unvaried grey eucalyptus bush, dry wheat lands and beaten earth that stretched beyond the gate, for it was a garden of incredible shades of bright colour in an often climatically hostile environment. To enjoy this growing marvel all eyes had to be kept on the flowers themselves, for the beds in which they grew were carefully covered with bulky rotted straw

... many of today's roses bred in cool temperate climates need copious water.

mulch, and paths of baked earth were obliterated by multiple tramlines of hoses. Once temporary, but now apparently permanent, protective structures covered cool temperate treasures to allow the longed-for glamour of hydrangeas, camellias and azaleas. I know that from sunrise until the mosquitoes sent everyone indoors the hoses were constantly moved to keep the garden alive, and the vision was sustained to the constant drone of the pump.

Although this garden was kept going through the sheer tenacity and dedication of the gardener, the majority of the chosen plants were quite incorrect for a climate subject to long, dry spells. However, the flipside of keeping gardens such as this alive was accepted without question for the reward of the green leaves or the simple solace of a row of pansies. This is the accepted norm for many a substantial garden whose original influences were 19th-century northern European. The favourite plants in that unsuitable Australian garden were roses, and these are a traditional flower for dry lands, but many of today's roses bred in cool temperate climates need copious water. In my dry garden, David Austin roses had to be given a bucket of water daily to perform, and when I saw hybrid tea roses growing in a historic garden in Aix-en-Provence I noticed they too grew between snakes of black hoses. So, although a genus may encompass a wide range of growing conditions, individual varieties can be place-specific, which should always be taken into consideration.

When considering resilient plants I have become fascinated by the range of sustainable plants for gardens from the Mediterranean climate zone through

Above: Nepeta in a border in the cool temperate garden of West Green House, but it would look just as good in a garden waiting for rain.

Below: The garden at Motissfont in Hampshire is the ultimate dream of an English garden in spring. Both the box hedge and the rose bushes would perform just as beautifully in a Mediterranean garden.

to a cool temperate garden. I am not evaluating desert plants or those at the extreme edges of the cool climate zone bordering on to the tundra regions. I am most interested in plants that can accept the cool temperate to Mediterranean zones, where summers can be five months of dry warm weather with days that can touch 35–40°C with as little as 60cm of rainfall annually, through to more temperate areas that know frosts can come at any time within a range of about five months and snow is expected in winter. And there will be variations, with more moisture towards the coast or rain-shadow pockets, or wind tunnels caused by local topography to influence regional weather. Among a truly international assemblage of plants we have the material to design gardens in the 21st century that will have the tenacity to withstand whatever climate extreme unfolds, as long as proper attention is given to water, soil and protection.

This is a vast climate range, but the plants I describe are those I have watched in years when southern

Australia experienced its worst fires in memory, then floods occurred in Queensland, New South Wales and Victoria, and deep snow isolated much of England. I have chosen a basic collection of plants not for the extreme edges of the climate zone, the tropics or lands that experience very severe winters or parched, desert conditions, but solid reliable plants that are brave in the punishing, see-sawing climates we are experiencing inbetween these zones.

I hovered over many plants which could have been in the eligibility list, but the remembrance and disappointment of how particular plants suffered trying to be courageous still lingers. These included hornbeams, *Carpinus* spp., and lime, *Tilia* spp., which defoliated annually as hot summers refused to depart, so I felt it better for all concerned, the gardener and the plant, to leave them just to where they are totally content.

So, this is a steadfast and personal list of the unsung heroes which have survived all the gardens I've planted in either hemisphere.

Above: The *Eremurus robustus* originated in the harsh steppes of Asia Minor. It grows equally well here in the English garden at West Green House as in a parched garden.

Left: In an ancient desert garden in Morrocco, shaded by olive and palm trees, seedling vegetables establish themselves.

Right: The olive trees give filtered shade to Iris species and cerinthe in this Greek garden, two herbaceous plants that would be at home in a cool temperate garden, but with more direct sunlight.

protection

Like a child, young plants need care and protection to establish, although as adults the plants we are discussing will withstand a range of punishing climates. If they begin life in a warmer climate, they'll need protection in early life from over-warm sun and hot winds, and they will need to become adapted to a rationed water supply. A seedling that begins life in a cooler area must be guarded from cold, bitter winds, frost and snow. In later life too, they will welcome the protection of a fence or wall, and water when the going gets tough.

In the eastern Mediterranean, where the climate can be extreme, archaeologists have shown us that the earliest productive gardens were well protected by walls and sustained by water brought to them via manmade channels. In Syria, from a high wall above a wadi, I watched a farmer in the deep shade of palm and olive trees transferring silt from an irrigation rivulet onto newly prepared garden beds. Adjacent columns of colossal Roman ruins built on an already ancient Silk Road rose from the barren rough sands of the desert. It was a timeless scene of man sustaining life by the

Young plants need care and protection to establish…

protection

interaction of shelter and moisture. In Puglia, Italy, small immaculate vegetable plots were established randomly under the olives in a landscape of white terraced rocks and nearly continuous grey olive trees. Although gardening in Syria and southern Italy may be far from the experience of most of us, what the gardeners here were following was exactly the same principle as my stretching a simple hessian cloth across a row of lettuce seedlings in southern New South Wales to protect them from intense heat, or planting small plants under glass in northern Europe. Young plants universally need protection from extreme conditions.

Ancient garden builders have left us with a myriad of ideas we can use to our advantage. Their cloistered walkways, courtyards, decorative pavilions, protected paths and garden houses are among gardening's most delightful architectural concepts and all can become safe sanctuaries to protect plants. At the same time, such structures give an intimacy to a garden, a human scale that can be adopted and adapted with pleasure into modern gardens. In old Damascene houses all the rooms open onto an enclosed courtyard where raised beds outlined with patterned tiles are home to roses and pools, all cooled by gentle fountains and shaded by fine trees. This is a totally protected and enclosed space. Similarly, in Marrakech's Medina, the traditional Riad houses open onto central courtyards where tiny fountains splash and the noonday heat is captured in the canopy of tall, often evergreen, orange trees that shelter the small beds and pots. If we are gardening in a hot climate, we need to create an artificial environment to give new plants protection from sunlight and strong winds.

Left: Shade houses were the epitome of Victorian luxury in colonial gardens. This one, built by the Dangar family, on Dangar Island, north of Sydney, gave shade for gardeners to grow a wide range of plants.

Whenever I have looked at a space for a new garden in Australia it has been a day with either roaring westerly skin-dehydrating winds or so hot that the view has been blurred by sweat in my eyes. Before commencing a new garden, the first planned element always has to be protection. In Tangier, in north Africa, I saw two *mashrabiyas* – small buildings simply made from closely spaced, turned wood covered in vines – one shaded a fountain, another flowering plants. Although in a vastly different architectural style, my grandmother's shade house in many ways imitated the idea of these Islamic buildings. In Victorian-era Australia, shade houses were high vogue, some as large and as elaborate as conservatories, others just sheds of narrowly spaced slats of timber, close enough to cast shade but open to the sky for any rain to penetrate. Planted with cooling creepers, perhaps a fern collection, a pool of water and garden seats, they provided shaded sanctuary for people and plants. The water feature was generally little more than an unattractive still pool of water, but it helped to create a little humidity that assisted the new growth. New plant cuttings and seedlings need shade to survive as direct sunlight quickly dries out new roots and leaves, so where the sun is relentless a shade house creates its own atmosphere for plants to establish and flourish.

Building for protection

In the cooler climate of Europe some of the most fashionable and 'swagger' buildings ever conceived followed the trend set by the fabled orangery at Versailles, with often eccentric as well as elegant buildings to protect rare plants. At Margam Park in Wales an orangery 97 metres long is described in Loudon's *Encyclopaedia of Gardening* (1822) as having '110 orange trees, several of which are eighteen feet in height and remarkably handsome'. Along with extensive sheltered walled gardens, many 19th-century British estates had extravagant glasshouses, with Sir Joseph Paxton's greenhouses for Chatsworth being perhaps the most famous. These were not only splendid buildings but also hives of production, their shelter allowing production of tender vegetables and exotic fruits for the table. On a domestic scale, as soon as more humble glasshouses became obtainable they were taken up by gardeners throughout the country, particularly popular for growing specialist plants and tomatoes.

I have built two plant-propagating areas in my life, one in the warmth of Dangar Island, north of Sydney, the other a very everyday greenhouse in Hampshire. My warm-climate potting tunnel was just a steel frame, covered with chicken wire, with benches on either side used in early spring to raise summer vegetable seedlings. Its cover planting created a world of pink-red brocade from early spring, the rapidly growing evergreen vine *Jasminum polyanthum* engulfing every space with a fragrant cloud of small, pale pink petals on deeper pink trumpets. Never watered, it needed only a hair clip after flowering and a good prune. This devastatingly fragrant jasmine is a greenhouse plant in cooler climates, but this family of climbers includes the hardy and resolutely resilient *Jasminum officinale* f. *affine*, scented with white flowers, that is suitable for a wider climate range. *Solanum*, often called the potato flower, climbed the tunnel's mesh in summer – not all varieties are hardy, but the purple-blue *Solanum crispum* 'Glasnevin' has a proven record in cooler areas. I admit a love-hate relationship with this plant, as it can become very straggly and show few flowers if it gets too much warmth and water. There was enough water on Dangar Island to grow *Hydrangea petiolaris* on the shady side of the tunnel, protecting its leaves from crisping. It flowers in a similar way to a lace-cap hydrangea, with large florets of creamy white, and I know it is a truly adaptable plant as I had one growing in nearly cool temperate Kennerton Green, 100 miles south of Sydney, while another flourishes on the coldest dark wall in Hampshire. All seemed equally content.

Autumn provided a magical mood in my warm-climate tunnel, when the ornamental grape vine, *Vitis coignetiae*, turned shades of vermilion, red and burgundy. It encased the entire structure, turning the interior into a rose-pink cave, especially in the rays of the late afternoon sun, giving shade in the hottest months. This is a generous plant that will endure a wide climate spectrum – it is equally resplendent dressing a Tudor barn along a West Green lane in autumn. My tunnel's plants were chosen for a succession of colour, planted closely enough to protect the seedlings and provide wind shelter, but all deciduous so the winter sun shone through.

Opposite left: The *hydrangea petiolaris* is suprisingly resilient, flowering both in deep shade and direct sun.

Opposite right: Grapevines in the greenhouse at West Green House.

Below: Established grapevines trained to a pagoda give summer protection.

Protective climbers

Vines are synonymous with shade and protection.
Sitting in cool sunlight under naked strands of a
well-clipped grapevine provides an inspiring albeit
clichéd image of hot countries, the remembered bliss
of a simple pole structure with a canopy of deep
green leaves and hands of grapes ripening on long
late summers' days. Fruiting vines, *Vitis vinifera*, are
long-lived plants given sun, good drainage and some
water to ensure fruit, but early frosts can hit the harvest
and an annual autumn pruning is essential. Incredibly
adaptable plants, vines will grow from Scandinavia to
the Sahara when grafted onto an appropriate regional

rootstock, so consult a local nursery about the most productive regional varieties. A northern-hemisphere gardener needs to provide them with a south-facing position and the protection of a nearby wall, and plant a proven variety. They have grown well outdoors for me in the UK where they are given as much warmth as possible, with good drainage, their roots thickly blanketed in perennial thyme to keep them warm, and we don't give them too rich a mulch. I've planted *Vitis* 'Fragola' with small tight bunches of grapes, and *Vitis vinifera* 'Incana' with deeply coloured fruit. *V. vinifera* 'Dornfelder' has stunning autumn leaf colour and red grapes.

I do have a purpose-built glasshouse in Hampshire in which I grow some of the more tender varieties – this working building certainly lacks the panache of my grandmother's shade house, but although it is not an elegant conservatory, it is pleasant to work in, attractive and functional. To festoon the crossbeams I am training *V. vinifera* 'Lakemont', a white grape with large bunches of green-yellow fruit, a recommended variety for the greenhouse or conservatory. Greenhouses even in cool regions become very warm on bright summer days and a vine's green leaves are welcome protection. The broad leaves of an espaliered fig growing in the warmth of a greenhouse give the same protection, as will the leaves of tender nectarines, peaches and apricots. Figs are in fact surprisingly hardy, and will also grow very successfully and produce delectable fruits outside in cool climates sheltered only by walls. *Ficus carica* 'Brown Turkey' is an excellent resilient variety. As a child in Australia, I considered the fig tree the best tree of all, for at sundown it looked as if its low-growing branches were covered with wide white flowers as its limbs provided the perfect roosting spot for the family's white hens.

Above left: The palmate leaves of an established fig tree.

Above: *Wisteria sinensis* cascades from a colonial cottage in New South Wales.

The sound of bees, the pervasive perfume and the froth of lavender racemes on a warm spring morning bring me nostalgic memories of homestead verandas draped in wisteria, of an old summerhouse that would have collapsed if its wisteria curtains were removed. The giant parasol of the glorious specimen of *Wisteria sinensis* that grew in my garden at Kennerton Green, Mittagong, did admittedly benefit from a garden bordering on to a cool climate, but wherever my life has led I've grown wisterias. I have planted gardens from the warm edge of the Mediterranean climate zone to a sub-tropical garden, and two in cool-climate regions, with my English garden in a very low-lying spot. Wisterias are the most glamorous of plants and have proved reliable, among the best deciduous shading vines. Because the racemes look so fragile, gardeners in warmer climates worry they need copious water, and those in cooler climates worry they require heat, but once established they need very little – just look around old gardens and you will see them abandoned but still flowering, relying on whatever nature delivers.

New wisteria plants do need attention, and the plants like some warmth and prefer, if possible, wind protection, but I have discovered for myself that many are decidedly unfaddish. Growing them alongside paths to form tunnels in warm gardens where gravel has crept into their soil, giving excellent drainage, they have flowered splendidly. The ethereal white *W. floribunda* 'Alba' that drapes Minerva's bust high on the south side of West Green House also grows in gravel, but the entrance to the walled garden here is nearly concealed by a wisteria that is known to be a century old, flourishing in an established border that is both

... wherever my life has led I've grown wisterias

mulched and watered. When I planted three wisterias on the cool, south side of a barn at Kennerton Green in a new bed they grew quickly, but put out excessive leaf and few flowers, so really I find they are plants that flout the rules.

Wisterias are strong vines requiring solid supports. When the walled garden at West Green was being remade, I asked the workmen to salvage any material that could reveal the garden's history. Late one afternoon I wandered down to check on the finds to discover the rusted remains of an extremely decorative iron arch, probably Victorian, embedded in wisteria wood. The strength of this vine had been immense. Wisterias can be trained across arches or up walls, and make excellent pot plants when the main stem is twisted around a firm stake until it forms a long, rigid trunk. The stake can be the base of a frame to drape the branches into an umbrella form. I made these in huge containers for each corner of a pool at least two decades ago and recently looking through a current UK plant catalogue I saw a promotional picture for wisteria and there were my Australian pots – I was totally flattered. Wisterias send out long, loose shoots after flowering, which can be snipped to tidy them back, but the main pruning should be in the plants' dormant period. Late, sharp frosts can be lethal to forming buds and knock out a season's flowering, yet they will perform again the following year. Always buy a wisteria in flower as seedlings are unreliable and may never flower properly. If a new wisteria has not flowered after a couple of seasons, let it go, for I do not believe it ever will.

Perhaps the most imperious of all the creepers is the climbing honeysuckle, Lonicera. Scattered with flowers, many varieties are sweetly scented and all grow speedily – some may even grow too fast if they are given rich soil, moisture and a sunny spot. In little over one season they can start to form a dead twiggy thatch that detracts from their beauty and is laborious to remove. Not being

Left: Whichever *Lonicera* variety you chose, it will be resilient with just the minimum of care.

Perhaps the most imperious of all the creepers is the climbing honeysuckle, *Lonicera*

temperamental, honeysuckles will accept warm and cool climates with minimal water; like wisterias they also need strong supports and they can make attractive pompom trees by twisting their main stem around a very firm stake to form a trunk, and pruning the head. *Lonicera periclymenum* 'Belgica' is a sorbet confection of cream, purple and red, perfect planted in a bed of just pink flowers to take away the too-pretty look. There is a huge range of honeysuckles including fragrant, deciduous and evergreen; some have leaves with coloured margins and flowers in cream, yellows, golds, reds, oranges, pinks and exhilarating bi-colours. But sometimes a resilient plant given too much of a good thing can become a garden or an environmental thug. In many parts of the USA *Lonicera japonica* is classified as an invasive weed. Likewise *Verbena bonariensis*, whose pink-purple flowers held high on tall slender stems can give desired movement to a late-season English border, is also a rogue in the Australian countryside. Similarly the brilliant small florets of *Lantana*, so admired in a Spanish window box, are the curse of the Australian rainforests. These are plants beyond resilient in particular areas.

Resilient creepers have also always acted as a form of living air conditioning and insulation for houses both in warm temperatures and where the weather is bitter. Hardy European climbers can be as effective on dwellings in drought-prone regions as on traditional European houses. Dense vines, especially ivies, *Hedera* spp., and Boston ivy, *Parthenocissus tricuspidata*, are most often used to protect a house's fabric from extreme heat or driving rain and tempest, but my old Hampshire house has a living palisade of *Magnolia grandiflora* pruned to be a protective green wall planted beside its foundations. Tolerant species protect the masonry from heat, and vines hanging from wide verandas act as filter curtains to cool the air and capture dust. In the days before air conditioning, as the mercury rose, green vines covering our veranda in New South Wales made it the cool heart of the house where we gossiped, ate and slept, and as dusk fell the largest, hairiest spiders imaginable became silhouetted each evening there in their large webs, spreading from the vine tendrils. There was always a debate, whether to let them and their fly-trapping webs stay, or be disposed of, but inevitably, whatever the decision, by evening their cousins plus small frogs, a toad, summer moths and beetles came too. It did not matter how many spiders were got rid of, more were rehearsing to take over. I smile when garden writers rhapsodise about how to attract wildlife to our gardens. Of course they are encouraging bumble bees, butterflies and birds, but it's hard to forget the other garden inhabitants of hot nights in warm climates!

Protective shrubs and trees

Formal and informal hedges or dense plantings are wind and dust protectors that can create microclimates to provide sanctuary for plants and people. In fire-prone areas, green plants that are not combustible can be used to form a green oasis to help as a fire barrier. The white cedar, *Melia azedarach*, (not a tree for cool gardens) and Portuguese laurel, *Prunus lusitanica*, both have some resistance to fire. The elegant, deciduous honey locust, *Gleditsia triacanthos*, with leaves like ferns, is a must-have resilient tree for larger gardens and, when cut as a hedge, it has a light and airy feeling and is therefore very effective and not overpowering in a smaller space. Although some of the trees have vicious spiny thorns, two of the best are friendly thornless varieties, both preferring an exposed sunny position to show off their colour. *G. triacanthos* 'Sunburst' is a pale golden-green in spring which gradually turns a deeper shade to reach a translucent gold in autumn; *G. triacanthos* 'Rubylace' has bronze-red leaves.

Left: Magnolia grandiflora has formed a protective palisade of leaves against a wall at West Green House in Hampshire.

Right: The Gleditsia triacanthos 'Sunburst' is a tree that will give golden resilience.

Some attractive shrubs that grow contentedly in both cool and warm climates make hedges suitable for gardens of any size. The dramatic dark-leafed smoke bush, *Cotinus coggygria*, with its wine-purple leaves and autumn colour, is truly hardy. Although it is grown primarily for its rich leaf colour, its hazy summer flowers give a delightful cloud cover to the plant – a contrast from the heavier feeling of some hedges. *Cotinus* is as tolerant of snow, wet and long periods of cold as it is of drought and snap frosts, and best of all it is long-lived. Among many varieties, warm-climate catalogues suggest *C. coggygria* 'Velvet Cloak', while a cooler-climate recommendation is *C. coggygria* 'Royal Purple'.

With tassels so long they would be the envy of a burlesque dancer, *Garrya elliptica* is a useful evergreen shrub which grows slowly to about 3m and comes into its own when the weather is chilly and the garden bare, producing giant silvery catkins that stay on the plant for months. In a warm climate, I grew it partly in dappled shade and on a gentle slope that gave natural drainage. A hedge of garrya at West Green House does have the protection of a barn where I've found it resilient in cold winters, but some friends query this. The drainage at West Green House is just average; however, drainage is important. Whether you grow them as individual shrubs or keep them compact as a hedge, the interesting form of these plants is an added bonus to their extreme functionality.

Formal hedging in shades of green forms the bones of gardens large and small in any climate, its structural elegance creating the garden background theatre. *Viburnum tinus* is a dense shrub with fists of white flowers in late winter emerging from pink buds, evergreen with rough, tough-looking, oval leaves. It will grow to 3m tall, so can be cut into a hedge of good height. I have *V. tinus* clipped as tall lollipops outlining paths in the UK, and plants have certainly coped with a southern New South Wales summer. The

Opposite: These tassles of *Garrya elliptica* are the envy of any burlesque dancer. This is a plant that makes the most interesting hedge.

Top left: Tough, undemanding and beautiful in spring, the laurustinus, *Viburnum tinus*.

Bottom left: The beautiful near aqua-blue of *Cupressus arizonica* var. *glabra* 'Blue Ice' deserves a place in the garden.

Right: The Portuguese laurel withstands so many climate extremes that it is invaluable in a resilient garden.

Formal hedging in shades of green forms the bones of gardens large and small …

protection

tall Portuguese laurel, *Prunus lusitanica*, survives a vast range of climates, but its large glossy green leaves are so imposing I'm not sure I would introduce it in a small garden, although it grows contentedly in either sun and shade, survives on whatever rain it receives, and has perfumed, creamy white flowers.

Cupressus, in many guises, creates evergreen structure in warm-climates, but yew is a preferred choice for many cooler gardens. The tall columnar Italian cypress, *Cupressus sempervirens*, can be grown either as a stately column or cut to form solid hedges from the Mediterranean climate zone to cooler regions. A long line of *Cupressus arizonica* var. *glabra* 'Blue Ice', with glorious muted greeny blue foliage, grew along a bed backed by a wall in the New South Wales Southern Highlands.

Establishing shelter for plants helps to combat wind so the soil's moisture is preserved and the plants can concentrate on establishing the roots they need for survival. A screening thicket, less solid than a dense hedge planting, can be created by close planting of a group of trees of suitable size for the garden. Many urban streets are virtual wind tunnels, so in towns trees can be planted to filter wind as well as providing some assistance as noise barriers, and of course they are often used to screen an urban view. Wind can also burn leaves, drying them out and tossing them around. Although a sharp controlled hedge will screen and protect, I like the special quality of trees, whose colour and form will create a garden's character. I've always thought a garden just of suitable plants personifies civic correctness – in the world we live in today, when 'those that know' at the Town Hall remove large trees because they are invasive or could cause 'health and safety' problems and replace them with small trees, it results in the trees having no impact against the mass of urban buildings.

Establishing young trees
Young trees, even nursery-established specimens, will need their own protection while they get established in a garden. A perforated plastic sleeve keeps nibbling creatures at bay and a firm stake attached to the tree by a wide strap will anchor the plant from tormenting wind, ensuring straight growth and stability for the new root system to develop. In hot climates, early protection can be rather different. In Australia I remember a dense planting of quick-growing, short-lived nursery trees, a thicket of omalanthus and acacias, growing as a wind and shade protection barrier for a new grove of lemon-scented gums, *Eucalyptus citriodora*. The use of rapidly maturing native trees to engulf new test-tube-grown seedlings is a conventional practice. They act as nurserymaid trees, their filtered shade helping to retain any moisture, and their short lifespan of 7–15 years corresponds with the maturing of the young trees. When nursery trees are planted as tiny seedlings at the same time as the future specimen trees, both acclimatise quickly. And when the nursery trees are removed, the new line of specimen trees has established a deep root system to withstand the elements. Trees grown in tubs that could have been used to establish an avenue rarely achieve such a deep root system as those grown in open ground.

Trees protecting flowers
Warm-climate gardens tend not to look like many northern, cool temperate ones. I remember, when two famous English gardeners came to my garden in Australia, how I proudly showed them our over-watered, fed and pampered spring displays, huge bands of ranunculus, anemones, primulas and stocks flowering under the large trees just beginning to come into leaf. Early spring when the air was cool was our time for these flowers, three months when everything came at once. They were among a long list that went on to daffodils and peonies in abundant parade, then stopped as the vast canopy came into leaf and covered nearly the entire garden. As good visitors the English gardeners said nothing, but later I learnt they were shocked at the idea of interlocking trees over

Opposite: Old pines in an Italian garden offer dappled shade to miniature cyclamen, a beautiful hardy ground cover.

beds because, in their north European experience, for flowers to perform well they have to have the maximum warmth of the northern hemisphere's weaker sun. The absence of perennials in these midsummer borders relying on just shade-tolerant shrubs made my warm-climate garden unexpected.

It is totally possible to grow a magnificent herbaceous border in a warm, dry climate by choosing a suitable range of perennials, but to grow they must have reasonable exposure to the sun just as in a north European border, so the gardener must make the choice – either flowers in spring with giant shade trees covering everything and everyone in summer, or brilliant flowers with minimum shade. Many gardeners choose divided gardens with trees covering the dwelling and hedges around a flower garden further away, but where space is tight it has to be either or.

Trees give a garden individuality with their size, foliage and shape and their shade encourages humidity as well as a cooling atmosphere. *Tamarix parviflora* is an ethereal, filmy, small tree that grows throughout the Mediterranean with fine stems and pink flowers. I first saw it planted to stabilise sand dunes in desert country beyond Broken Hill in far western New South Wales, then again, softly pendulous, by a Syrian courtyard. In a garden in Provence it provided shelter for cerise-pink roses, giving a lesson in saturated colour. In one of the coldest spots on the pond bank at West Green House, a group of three tamarix have settled down happily. When they were first planted there, their roots only a few feet above the water's edge, I surmised that they would not grow, but obviously there is enough drainage and warmth for them to flower, so I insist they are super-class resilient. Only 4m tall, this small tree looks at its best grown in groups. *T. tetrandra* flowers in spring and *T. ramosissima* in autumn.

Romantically named golden rain trees, *Koelreuteria* spp., are thought to have inspired the willow pattern china designs. With sprays of yellow flowers and fruit resembling Chinese lanterns, this 10m tree is suitable

Trees give
a garden
individuality
with their
size, foliage
and shape …

Right: Robinia pseudoacacia 'Frisia' is a
favoured street tree in Sydney's
seaside suburbs. Here it is placed
in a border at West Green House.

Opposite top: These golden ash
leaves were photographed in the
RHS garden at Wisley, but these
trees were among the first choices
for my dry garden in southern
New South Wales.

Opposite bottom: The claret ash grew
in my family's garden in southern
New South Wales, but in an
English garden, it is performing
just as well

for most sized gardens and grows well in warm and cool climates, nurtured in composted, well-drained soil in an open position. *Robinia pseudoacacia* 'Umbraculifera' is an excellent urban tree, its softly rounded canopy adding bright green lightness to a garden, and appreciating the shelter of a building to protect it from wind. As long as its roots are well drained it will grow just about anywhere – perhaps the finest I've seen was in a garden in the Austrian Tyrol. However, its charm does hide a few sins – it's thorny and it will sucker freely. *R. pseudoacacia* 'Frisia' has limey gold leaves; I have one at West Green House and it's also a street tree in two New South Wales neighbourhoods I have called home.

Another golden-leafed tree that captures and defuses glowing light is the superb golden ash, *Fraxinus excelsior* 'Aurea'. Deciduous, spreading and relatively fast-growing to around 15m, it is a tree to be relied on. Although native to northern Europe, *Fraxinus* spp. are attuned to a wide climatic range: the narrow-leafed desert ash, *F. oxycarpa*, and the Syrian ash, *F. syriaca*, are reliable in dry areas and the claret ash, *F. angustifolia* 'Raywood', is adaptable in a wide climatic range: its foliage glowing burgundy in afternoon light. These are best as perimeter trees in drier areas as their roots tend to come to the surface to find water, and they will happily lift paving in their search.

Avoiding heatstroke

Warm-climate courtyards can be ovens at midday. Pergolas covered with deciduous climbing plants and their walls broken by vines offer welcome sanctuary in high summer. Contemporary courtyards covered with marble, granite and other light-reflective, hard surfaces can be the worst offenders, often generating truly terrible heat causing desert extremes that few plants will survive other than agaves, yucca or other species from arid lands. Hard-landscaped terraces should, for this reason, be as wide as practical to allow space for shading trees or vine-covered arches or walkways.

The courtyard is a traditional feature to provide protection from cold winds and frosts, allowing cool-climate gardeners some sheltered warmth to nurture their plants. Here the reflected heat of a wall can perhaps be used to espalier a more tender fruit tree, such as a peach or nectarine, but in a warm climate the same protective walls trap heat and need to be shaded, preferably by the canopy of a widely branched tree. A good choice is one of the most fetching

Left: A Moroccan courtyard protects green plants from summer's heat and is cooled by a small fountain.

and complacent of trees, the strawberry tree, *Arbutus unedo*, which comes from the western Mediterranean. Understated but decorative, it is a tough tree which can grow up to 6m tall with a wide and dense canopy above a beautiful trunk. Rough-textured fruit the size and colour of ripening strawberries follow the previous season's small white flowers. Arbutus will also grow happily in cooler climates, but may not fruit.

Cold protection

Coming from a warm climate, I found that protecting a garden from heat was second nature to me, but when I arrived in England I had to embrace the problems of protection from frozen ground, hoar frosts and snow. Years ago, surrounded by deep snow in a village in northern Japan, I saw how Japanese gardeners had immaculately bound their trees in rope and covered their plants with coarse cloth to protect them from the ravages of winter. It was a beautiful art form that I'd admired as a curiosity. Most of the winters I had experienced in Europe until recently had given little more than one or two good falls of snow a year, and a brisk turn around the garden dusting it off topiaries, clipped hedges and wide-leafed plants had kept the plants safe. Frosts were coped with by winding frost-tender plants like the culinary bay trees in white, frostproof fleece, so they looked like those half lemons wrapped and fetchingly tied in muslin that sometimes

appear in fashionable restaurants. In the greenhouse, plants had survived with plastic bubble wrap or frostproof fleece laid across them and a blow heater turned on when the weatherman recommended.

However, these last winters have been colder and snow deeper. To help topiaries, not only has the snow cover been brushed off, but firmer stakes have also been installed to support the trunks. The skills of those long-forgotten Japanese gardeners have re-entered my mind and I wished I had their knowledge of how to deal with weeks of intensive snow, for its weight breaks branches and garden buildings alike. I now make sure that columnar cypresses are tied up in twine like parcels and stone statues and glazed garden pots bundled up in hessian.

When I first came to England this white fluff everyone called frost cloth or fleece was a new phenomenon. The fleeces made today are of translucent, lightweight, synthetic fibres and porous to allow the plants to breathe. Different weights are available and, if harsher winters continue, heavier grades will be needed to cover susceptible plants while more resilient subjects are established. A thick cover of mulch around plant roots also provides good snow protection, and a thicket of branches makes a blanket to stop the earth beneath freezing – a farmer's advice that really works.

Bellow: At West Green House, old walls give protection from harsh winters and in summer these interior walls give warmth to fruiting fig trees.

protection

Designing with resilient favourites

Even in her last hours, my mother was still thinking about future plans for a woodland planting, and now I wonder if I may follow family tradition as visions of new tree plantings dance in my head. I know my next garden will be a small, enclosed one and I think I see it surrounded by an arbour to walk, sit or work beneath. This will be of a similar design to the pagoda I created to enclose a building at Kennerton Green, with cement columns and wide wooden crossbeams that were trained with *Clematis montana* var. *alba* and *Rosa* 'Wedding Day'. This robust and strong rose is single with champagne buds in clusters; the clematis was suitable for a climate that, although classified as cool temperate, ranged from zero to 35°C (95°F) but it did have summer water – I could otherwise have had drought-tolerant *Clematis* 'Golden Tiara'.

In a new garden, the branches of the Judas tree, *Cercis siliquastrum*, will be trained to a new arbour. I was inspired by a line of Judas trees pruned to a rustic wooden arbour across a pathway in southern France on a spring afternoon, the glowing cerise-pink flowers attached directly to the branches flowering when most of the early spring blossoms were gone and before the flush of roses and perennials. In France, the filtered shade was deep and cool beneath the arched walkway, for it was also protected on one side by a dry stone

> I was inspired by a line of Judas trees pruned to a rustic wooden arbour across a pathway in southern France on a spring afternoon…

wall, and many plants were nurtured in the shade. In fact the Judas tree is a very forbearing tree; a large specimen grows for me at West Green House. Mine does have the corner position in the walled garden, but success is reported from a colder and wetter Cotswold garden where these trees flower profusely every year, also trained to a pergola.

My planting beneath will be tough perennials able to thrive in the widest climate variations, reflecting the colours of the flowering trees. I will have succulent leaves of sedums for autumn, *Sedum telephium* (Atropurpurem Group) 'Purple Emperor', with pink-red flowers on purple foliage, and *S. telephium* 'Chocolate', with its new green leaves that deepen to chocolate behind deep pink flowers.

Below, left to right: Cercis siliquastrum; Sedum 'Purple Emperor'; Bergenia 'Bressingham White'; Dianthus.

A saxifrage grew in my mother's garden in the Mediterranean climate zone of southern New South Wales, its roots firmly embedded in a dry stone wall supporting an established bed. Sweet pink in colour, it was one of the first winter flowers to arrive. I am not certain of its variety, but an identical one grew in a similar position in the cool temperate Southern Highlands of New South Wales, a hundred or so miles inland from Sydney, and older reference books indicate it may have been *Bergenia cordifolia* (from the same family). The walls retained some moisture there, but these plants enjoy the sun and accept clay, sandy and alkaline soils. *Bergenia* 'Bressingham White' is a recommended form, with pale flowers held above leaves that colour well in winter. *B.* 'Wintermärchen' is renowned for its disregard for climate, its glossy red-purple winter leaves

protection

followed by deep rose spring flowers. On my visit to Sweden, where winter is truly winter, the elephant-ear leaves of bergenias were a common sight as ground cover, growing in shallow soil above rocky terrain. I know I will have to leave my chair from time to time to remove their ugly spent leaves, but they are worthwhile plants, behaving beautifully in both dry and cool temperate gardens.

Although associated with traditional north European cottage gardens, *Dianthus*, on thin wiry stems, are sun-loving and drought-tolerant, making exceptional edging plants. I'd introduce their neat tussocks of grey leaves with double and single flowers, perhaps some with deep eyes, speckled and picotee-edged in every shade from dark maroon through sugar pink to white. They withstand English cold, and long, hot summers in well-drained beds or pots where their clove perfume lingers in the air on warm evenings. Along with the biennial, dark Sweet William, *Dianthus barbatus* 'Sooty', and its pure black velvet flowers, tones of hot pinks through to the black would make a dream garden.

In northern Europe, lilacs are common around fields and gardens. Armfuls of their huge and deliciously scented panicles of massed purple, lavender, mauve, pink and white colonise vases in early summer. Many popular floriferous hybrids do prefer a cooler temperature, although they seem to perform well after a sunny spring. Persian lilac, *Syringa* x *persica*, is a superb form, sweetly scented and attractively drooping, but equally pretty and thoroughly resilient is its relative *S. wolfii*, a Korean native growing to 4m. This lilac will contend with drought and cold once established and, if grown in a small grove, will provide a beautiful springtime thicket to mask the outside world. In my cool temperate garden I grow *S.* x *persica* surrounded with plants with silvery leaves – *Scabiosa caucasica* with its mauve-blue ruffled pin-head cushions heads above frilled silvery leaves, and the furry grey leaves

and ruby faces of rose campion, *Lychnis coronaria*. In a hotter dry climate, I might keep these plants or would add a carpet of the silvery-leafed evergreen *Salvia officinalis* 'Berggarten' and introduce the rounded 45cm clumps of shrubby horehound, *Ballota pseudodictamnus*, whose soft, thick, rounded leaves are a must in any dry garden. I would keep the look I like simply by changing the variety of the main subject, in this case substituting a tougher lilac.

To capture and repeat their tones, the underplanting at West Green House includes the polyantha rose, *Rosa* 'Rhapsody in Blue', with clusters of violet, fuschia and grey shades with silver provided by *Eryngium giganteum* 'Silver Ghost', as sharp and as icy as Narnia's witch, and the feathery silver leaves of *Centaurea*. This perennial cornflower can be white, pink, lilac or blue and is suitable for poor soils and neglect. The roses and the eryngiums both like good well-drained soil and summer water, but they will sanction a wide range of climates.

Clockwise, from far left: Syringa persica; Lynchis coronaria; Ballota psudodicatmnus; mixed cornflowers (Centaurea cyanus); Salvia officinalis 'Berggarten'; Scabiosa caucasica; Dianthus barbatus 'Sooty'

Right: An Asian Buddha gazes out across the cool waters of a seaside garden in Tasmania.

water

...if we are to continue gardening we have to re-evaluate this inherited style of gardening...

Water in warmer climates is always a primary topic, either for its lack or its over-abundance. Already in marginal lands in Australia farming has been abandoned and in some areas drought has been so long and severe that cities legislated against the paying of water features, fountains and rills and daytime garden watering was banned. Friends in southern Australia used to set their alarm clocks for midnight and beyond on their allotted watering days, trusting that by then there would be pressure enough in the hose pipe for hand watering – the days of using sprinklers was long past. Then in early 2011 came a devastating flood, fiercer than any for 100 years. But despite the ever-changing unpredictable weather, many gardeners in Australia, New Zealand, South Africa and California, even expats designing gardens along the Mediterranean seashore, continue to garden in the north European way. Although the style came out of a cool temperate land (a 19-century English garden style), it has been transferred to some of the world's hottest climates unadulterated, a style basically unsuited to drier environments as it demands lawns, shrubs and exotic trees backing banks of perennials and annuals, their beauty often reflected in ornamental water.

Opposite: Rills of water in a traditional Islamic style garden cools the air in coastal Morrocco.

Above: The theatre lawn at West Green House.

Left: To keep this lawn verdant and green in Bowral in New South Wales it had to be watered regularly in summer.

These English- and north European-style gardens continued to succeed quite admirably in some unlikely climates through much of the 20th century, when winter brought rains to harsher areas, and by spring the gardens were masses of flowers, with their planting adapted over time to substitute many hardier South African and Mediterranean species for the European originals. Now for more than a decade the rains have become unreliable and weather patterns unexpected and severe, so if we are to continue gardening we have to re-evaluate this inherited style of gardening and take a long look at exactly how much water each area of a garden consumes, and whether it can be justified.

Lawns

Lawns are not part of a resilient garden but everyone wants one. They are my *bête noire*, for they always seem to have difficulties. Recent long, hot, dry summers in both Europe and the southern hemisphere have meant the lawns looked dry and unattractive by midsummer. For a warm-climate gardener this has been an annual problem – if you sow a warm-climate variety of grass seed they look grey and dull in winter and vice versa. For nine months of the year they need a weekly mow, then edging, weeding and feeding. Brown spots occur regularly (and in England, where I can't always blame the weather, brown molehills arrive one day ahead

of guests). Even when there is water, as the heat of midsummer builds up it is nearly impossible to keep even an over-tended lawn in either climate in good condition. Regardless of an early-morning watering, the moisture evaporates quickly in the heat, and then as summer progresses water supplies are limited or non-existent. When it was a perfect day to sit out in Australia the lawn was typically crispy beige, the only green patches the burrs of bindi, *Soliva pterosperma*, a weed lethal to bare feet.

When I arrived at West Green House, the question of lawns could not be ignored, for there was buttercup-infested grass in the walled garden and, where the verdant terraces of our sloping theatre lawns now begin, a glasshouse's remains were hidden by waist-high grass. First, the long grass was slashed and then mown, stubborn buttercups were blitzed by hand using a long sharp knife to the roots, then fine sand and loam were mixed with a recommended seed mix and spread in autumn. Soft English rain fell, a new mower with sharp blades arrived and perfect green stripes have since been cut across it every year once a week from late March to nearly November. But within the first season another menace appeared – moss – necessitating a new de-mossing regime of de-thatching, aerating and controlling with selective herbicide.

… as the heat of midsummer builds up it is nearly impossible to keep even an over-tended lawn in either climate in good condition

Alternatives to grass

Lawns may provide desirable spaces of calm simplicity, but there are more resilient alternatives, such as framing our houses on the street sides with drought-resistant groundcover plants trailing across stone or paved areas to provide colour, texture and flower. Colour can create many atmospheres, and many suitable groundcover plants will make a sea of blue and silver-grey, a desirable alternative to the inevitable lawn where there is not enough water to sustain midsummer green. Furry silver-grey lamb's ears, *Stachys byzantina* 'Silky Fleece', make a compact mat when given minimal water. Over three hundred thyme species are ideal low-maintenance ground covers; woody thyme, *Thymus pseudolanuginosus*, grows just 1cm high and creeps and mats. *Thymus citriodorus* is dense and low-growing and releases a lovely lemon scent when walked across. Cover any mound or wall with evergreen and aromatic low-growing rosemary, *Rosmarinus officinalis* 'Prostratus', and *Convolvulus sabatius* trails small, lavender-blue, moon-shaped flowers over grey leaves.

Hot weather can be matched with hot, rather than cool, colours. The painter Monet let annual sun-loving nasturtiums in oranges and yellows cover plants and gravel paths alike from late summer to the frosts. Monet's garden in front of the old house in France has no lawn, just jewel-coloured flowers surrounded by gravel. Today nasturtiums in colours from cream to mahogany red, many with mottled leaves, will grow with limited water and spread themselves merrily — once nasturtiums are planted you have them forever, for they seed and reseed. For a difficult stony area that needs a blanket from spring into early summer, the humble poached egg plant *Limnanthes douglasii*, provides a light green mat studded with thousands upon thousands of yellow and white faces. As spring begins to warm it is crisp and inviting, surviving between rocks or in the gravel and existing on just spring rain when it comes. It's the perfect annual that can be pulled out and tossed away when flowering ends, but come next spring it simply returns as it is a wilful self-seeder like the nasturtium.

Sedum 'Bertram Anderson' makes a thick carpet to rival any aristocratic one, and like good floor covering it looks best growing in substantial drifts. For most of the season it masquerades as a textured dusty purplish collection of self-effacing leaves that fade into the atmosphere, but in autumn it electrifies

Bellow, left to right: Limanthes douglassi; swirls of Santolina; Sedum 'Bertram Anderson'.

Opposite: This is my idea of how to eliminate lawns, replacing it with a design of great beauty. Here, lamb's-ear (Staychs byzantina), chives are far more resilient than ever a lawn could be.

Box is one of gardening's most refined plants, it's always green and can be clipped into almost any shape …

into large heads of rich pink flowers. It was for me too humble to be a front-of-the-border plant because viewed from a distance, it seems to disappear, but it is an excellent plant to dress a difficult slope. Just plant the sedum into a good layer of mulch; it will need very little water and accept whatever the elements bring. These plants not only need so much less water and management than lawns, but they also make a cool or fiery-coloured frame for the home.

Too often we try to sow grass and strive to maintain it in areas more suited to alternative treatments. Instead of lawn, under the dry shade of an aged pin oak, *Quercus palustris*, in my Mittagong garden in Australia I laid out a fanciful low-growing green parterre, clipping hardy, small-leafed box, *Buxus sempervirens*, into swirls with clipped cone verticals. These thrived

in a position where grass simply could not survive. A zero water solution would have been to gravel this dry shade or to use bush rocks or terracotta tiles beneath the tree, but I did have enough winter and spring rain to promote growth with minimum summer supplement. To glamorise the design, hardy seedlings of granny's bonnets, *Aquilegia vulgaris*, were permitted to self-seed, along with mat-forming soft lavender-coloured daisies, *Brachyscome multifida*, adding colour to the strong green shapes. Box is one of gardening's most refined plants – it's always green and can be clipped into almost any shape, growing happily in sun, shade and with minimum water. The box transformed what had formerly been a shady problem area into one of the garden's most unexpected and enticing spots – in fact a garden seat arrived so it could be enjoyed in style.

Left: Here a garden has dispensed with grass either side of the path, planted instead with super-resilient hemercallis (right), which flowers throughout summer into autumn.

Opposite: In a French seaside garden where coastal conditions are not conducive to grass, geometric shapes, both in plant material and hard landscaping, give us a superb design.

Enhancing grass

In the northern hemisphere's cooler climate, good grasses seem to be waiting everywhere, yearning to be turned into lawns. To avoid endless lawn management, some grassed spots at West Green were encouraged to go wild with a wildflower and grass mix, here it was a clay mix with ox-eye daisy, *Leucanthemum vulgare*, predominating – there are also grass and wildflower mixes for chalky, clay, acid and wet soils. This is a late spring joy to be mown back in midsummer when it becomes rank. Bulbs lurk beneath the grass, and even when winter is at its drabbest there's a sublime procession waiting to come through. Crocus in the coldest months, in well-drained soil, just reappear each year with small flower cups in white or yellow, blue, striped and bicolour. Larger Dutch crocus can rival a species tulip in size, and do not need the cool of Europe – they delight in warmer climates as many are native to the Adriatic coast, Italy, Turkey and Greece. The purple-feathered *Crocus vernus* 'Pickwick', the lavender and blue C. 'Blue Pearl' with its prominent orange stigmas and C. *sieberi* 'Bowles White' are all very special and grow equally well in cool and dry, warm climates.

The tall white *Narcissus* 'Earlicheer', with yellow peeping through the petals and up to twenty flowers on a stem, grew for me as happily in New South Wales as it does in the UK, and the dwarf March daffodil 'Tête-à-tête', a free-flowering 23cm golden bulb, was just as content, but my favourite little yellow-hooped daffodil N. *Bulbocodium* subsp. *bulbocodium* var. *conspicuus* seems to prefer warmth because it sulks at West Green House while it was spectacular in Mittagong. Its small

Above: For 9 months of the year the lakeside at West Green House is a swathe of grass, but for three months in spring, it is enhanced by daffodils. Here are the late-flowering *Narcissus poeticus* var. *recurvus* 'Old Pheasant's Eye'.

Clockwise, from far left: Autumn-flowering *Colchicum*; *Crocus tomassinianus* flowering with snowdrops (*Galanthus*); lilac autumn-flowering *Colchicum*; *Crocus tomassinianus*.

Lilium martagon rise above the grass, growing up to 1m tall, continuing this succession of bulb magic

Left: Lilium martagon.

Opposite: The back door of West Green House opens up onto a gravel courtyard where box rings surround heritage apple trees.

yellow flowers multiply continuously and it dies back perfectly as its leaves are fine and unnoticed. (I skirt around the large-trumpeted traditional-form daffodils, including 'King Alfred', that happily grow from Norwegian cold to close to the sub-tropics, for as they die back they leave unsightly patches of browning foliage just as the garden is perfection elsewhere.) Then there is the white mass of *Narcissus* 'Mount Hood' and the unmissable May-flowering *N. poeticus* var. *recurvus* 'Old Pheasant's Eye', a sweetly scented, flat, white daffodil with a short, yellow, rose-edged trumpet with a darker rim. These are absolute musts for me in a bulb collection.

In quick succession come bluebells, *Scilla hispanica*, happy in climates from cool to dry, then the maturing grass is skimmed with blue Dutch iris, an everyday but dependable bulb, and finally the spotted Turk's cap or Martagon lilies, *Lilium martagon*, rise above the grass, growing up to 1m tall, continuing this succession of bulb magic for another three weeks. By mid-June these bulbs are mown away and, within three weeks, the grass is back to a mown sward for picnics and pleasure. Bulbs lurking beneath the grass are bonus plants, for they return in greater numbers each spring without watering, just quietly departing when the grass is required for summer enjoyment.

I've never wasted water on grass because if it browns in summer, at the first rains or with winter flooding it naturally returns. Thank goodness that even in England previous gardeners at West Green House did not overburden me with lawns, for on three sides of the house the doors open up on to gravel courtyards. One is decorated by box rings out of which heritage apple trees grow, another has a whimsical parterre of hearts, and the other is hedged with informal topiaries – all practical ideas to get round the problem of lawns and the water they use.

Ornamental water

It has been said that light-reflecting pools of water are the eyes of a garden, but coping with ornamental water in a hot climate is not easy, and not always practical or desirable. Evaporation means that features must be checked daily so there is sufficient water remaining for a pump to function. Even deep ponds demand to be topped up, which may not be an option when there are water shortages, while shallower water forms algae in intense sunlight, which must be removed constantly. Suggestions to prevent algal growth include submerging bales of barley straw in deep ponds and many chemical solutions. I've found that adding salt is helpful if there isn't any plant life. Algae-eating fish and oxygenating the water with aquatic verge planting are reasonable solutions, but even the best-planned aquatic plant groupings will relish the warm sun and water and become overwhelming, as invasive as any weeds. Tired of fighting it, I eventually let a white water lily swamp the surface of one entire pond, the wide pads covering the murky water beneath, and kept some control by lifting and subdividing the lilies every three years. Although it was one of the most tranquil water features I've made, it was only feasible a long way from the living area – it did attract wonderful dragonflies on summer days, but mosquitoes were always in season.

Small amounts of water are more desirable, easier to manage and provide. Inspired by the early Islamic builders throughout the Middle East and Mediterranean who used decorative water features to bring light, sound and pleasure into the centre of their buildings, I made an enclosed courtyard in my

Australian garden. In it rills were largely fed by recycled rainwater stored in a small underground tank and re-used, a submerged pump ensuring continuous flow. Water entered the garden in a variety of ways – down small spillways, slowly bubbling up into water basins or dripping from decorative spouts in walls, with serpentine rills meandering past softening plantings.

If we collect rainwater from our buildings we do not need to have gardens devoid of the softening sounds and look of water – a garden just of paving, gravel and suitable plants can be rather underwhelming. Think of the Court of the Lions at the Alhambra Palace in Spain with its small rills and basins of water, or the gossamer fountains along the Patio de la Acequia in the Generalife. Granted, these palace gardens are fed by old aqueducts that bring water from the melting snows of the Sierra Nevada, but the volume of water is far less than that required for a traditional north European deep pond or lake. We don't need to give up on water features where water is scarce; their value is immeasurable for the pleasure of the sound of water in still heat. A lazy jet of water spilling from an old urn into a reed-filled pond or into gravel and continuously recycled via a basic pump is a simple idea and easy to set up. Contemporary designs are no more complicated to install, such as water skimming glass, steel or mirror panels, water bubbling up in shallow dishes or a rill flowing between polished timber or marble.

Opposite: Irises grow in a country garden near Wagga Wagga in New South Wales, sustained only by winter rains and a pond that dries up during summer months.

Top left: Iris germanica rejoicing in the warmth from reflected gravel make a small body of water look more important.

Left: A tiny pond in the Mediterranean city of Tangier, creates cool atmosphere.

Plants by pools

In a world suffering from water shortages it may seem perverse to mention swimming pools, but in warm climates the swimming pool is ubiquitous, often taking up the entire yard – it is the meeting place of the family for most of the year. I appreciate when the words 'gardens' and 'swimming pools' are equated, it makes many gardeners shudder and definitely too many pools are just garish water-filled bright aqua holes surrounded by wall-to-wall concrete, but they can be as harmonious a feature as a stretch of ornamental water in a garden. In north Africa, encircled by sand-covered walls, I saw a grey slate-lined pool's perimeter decorated with locally made pots containing architectural grey agaves, the colours harmonising with the colours of the local landscape. In fact, the agave is the ultimate plant that doesn't need water. Within the shelter of a wall, *Agave* 'Americana' and the vivid striped yellow and green *A. variegata* will survive, and are so dramatic they look as if they have strayed from a prehistoric landscape.

Cordyline australis can provide similar drama and *C. australis* 'Red Sensation' and 'Purple Sensation' will even survive temperatures below freezing to -5°C (23°F). Phormiums triumph in harsh conditions as they don't object to either drought or cold, if sheltered from strong winds and protected with a blanket of mulch. *Phormium* 'Sundowner' is outstanding, with striped pink, purple and cream leaves. In Tangier, I saw a very everyday pool incorporated into a traditional Islamic courtyard of pools and gardens outlined in small streams of water. Rampant foliage covered the enclosing walls, but all eyes turned to the opulent-sized hibiscus, its tropical Hawaiian saucers in flashing colours.

But there are flamboyant hibiscus forms that are happy in many climates. A mass of these brilliant flowers planted in a Maryland, USA, coastal garden encouraged me to try one of these frost-hardy perennials that

Opposite: The inclusion of a traditional Islamic garden of rills and fountains makes an every-day swimming pool feel part of the garden's design.

Above: Hibiscus syriacus 'Bluebird'.

accept both cool and warm gardens when provided with a little water. Most of these cultivars originated in the extreme temperatures of midwest America. As red as its name, *Hibiscus* 'Fireball' grew superbly, with H. 'Moon Dance' in soft cream with a magenta eye, and bright pink H. 'Fantasia', all tolerating an Australian summer with no question. Flowering in midsummer makes them ideal forerunners for the later-flowering dahlias – they are of similar proportions and like similar conditions. The shrubby *Hibiscus syriacus* 'Bluebird' grows as successfully at West Green House as it did in a westerly exposed border in Victoria. Studded with flat lavender-blue flowers around dark eyes, this hibiscus can make a substantial hedge, happily flowering in the full sun of midsummer.

...there are flamboyant hibiscus that are happy in many climates...

Watering plants in containers

In some conditions only plants in containers will do, but watering pots is a science on its own. I have often wondered why summer flower colour is supplied so frequently only by annuals. Ruffled petunias, trailing pansies and lobelia are firm favourites, but they are all shallow-rooted annuals which are always thirsty and fragile, made even needier in free-standing pots that dry out in the summer sun or flood in rain. Quick-growing and colourful they may be, but I will never forget a carefully planned wedding where the mother of the bride had planted pots of white petunias and lobelia everywhere, then the evening before the ceremony a rain storm turned the petunias to pulp – the same bridal effect could have been sustained by a determined, climate-impervious daisy. The white marguerite, *Argyranthemum frutescens*, would have been perfect as it's an impeccable courtyard pot plant, forming an immaculate round head of white-petalled, yellow-centred flowers above grey-green leaves. It thrives in any soil, needs very little water and, if pruned after the first flowers are spent, will flower again by late summer.

White daisies in pots against a blue sky are an emblem of summer. The tall-stemmed shasta daisy, *Leucanthemum* x *superbum*, is another fully resilient white daisy. Numerous varieties have variously shaggy flowers, some pale lemon or semi-double, but all are capable of performing in the widest range of climate with some prudent water. And the low-growing golden marguerite, *Anthemis tinctoria*, with ferny leaves loiters to give repeat flowering if spent blooms are cut away; it likes a sunny position, good drainage and a long summer-flowering season – in fact it dislikes much water.

Euphorbias are excellent pot plants. I like blue, white and green plants beside water, echoing the serenity of the water and sky. *Euphorbia characias* 'Tasmanian Tiger' is a mass of cream-green bells above white-

I have often wondered why summer flower colour is supplied so frequently only by annuals…

Clockwise from far left: The maguerites, the bay tree (*Laurel nobilis*) and the Mediterranean herbs rosemary and lavender are the perfect pot plants in a resilient garden. Even after flowering, the rosemary and lavender still give elegant structure, if smartly clipped, and the evergreen laurel always looks good. The marguerite, if cut away after flowering, will give a second flowering within the season.

variegated leaves growing to 90cm tall. Blue can be supplied by herbs that are tremendously good pot plants – tough Mediterranean species that need dry feet and sun, dispersing their fragrance when you touch their leaves as well as via their flowers. There are so many suitable herbs, from the tall, highly aromatic, truly hardy English lavender, *Lavandula angustifolia*, with purple flowers growing to 1m, to its shorter relative *L. angustifolia* 'Munstead' with true lavender flowers growing to around 45cm, and numerous other varieties. I am enchanted by *L. stoechas* 'Tiara', a sapphire-blue flower topped by ears of creamy green. However, *stoechas* varieties are not entirely reliable and seem to like dappled sun, then within a few years they become scraggy and need to be replaced. Rue, *Ruta graveolens* 'Jackman's Blue', makes shiny mounds of rounded blue foliage around 70cm tall with a yellow flower, but some people do not like its scent. *Santolina* subsp. *rosmarinifolia* 'Primrose Gem' is a pale-green-leafed cotton lavender covered in small, pale lemon pompoms of flowers all summer; a winter haircut keeps it rounded for the following season.

Bright-flowering rosemaries are exellent in pots, especially *Rosmarinus officinalis* 'Gorizia' that grows in a similarly upright way to the ever-popular *R. officinalis* 'Miss Jessop's Upright', but with larger and bluer flowers. *R. officinalis* 'Mozart' reaches 1.2m tall and is literally smothered in deep blue flowers.

Agastache, a herb native to dry climates from China to North America, has 60cm vertical spikes topped with flowers in shades of apricot, pink, mauve, blue and white, while the similar-height rod-like stems of *Asphodeline lutea* are completely cloaked with sulphur-yellow flowers in summer. Both are drought-tolerant plants that look good in pots but are utterly resilient as they will grow in near-bog conditions just as happily.

Whether neglected in a rusty petrol can or pampered in good pots, the culinary bay tree, *Laurus nobilis*, is

Left: There is a yucca variety suitable for most resilient gardens. Their towering spikes of cream bells give the garden both beauty and structure.

Above: Agapanthus come in all shades of blue, from deep navy to the palest porcelain. They look magnificent in pots, giving not only superb flower but shiny strap-like leaves that arrange themselves in a tidy formation.

another plant for all climates and seasons. Cultivated, chic and tidy, it is ideal in courtyards or near poolsides as it keeps its dignity and scatters no leaves. In the harshest winters, in exposed positions, it needs to be wrapped in fleece, but is otherwise trouble free, and bay tree suckers can make controlled hedges in dry areas, as a bay tree will continually make new shoots if its roots are disturbed.

Despite their being regarded as desert plants, tall wands of cream yuccas look majestic in unwatered pots. Although their spikes make them unwise choices for plantings where people pass too closely, in the right spot they are such excellent candidates, with their arresting leaf shape and their complete disregard for care. *Yucca whipplei* is like a great ball of grey baguettes, with a flower spike 5m tall and a multitude of flowers like a cloud in the sky. In a sheltered warm spot in northern Europe it has grown quite well, and in hotter

If you're looking for resilient pot plants to withstand drought and soaring temperatures, a primary choice is agapanthus

areas it is a superb, complacent plant. Their grey shapes look well anchored placed near generously clipped balls of the evergreen Indian hawthorn, *Rhaphiolepis umbellata*, with its dark green leaves and tiny bunches of white flowers in late spring or early summer. The Indian hawthorn is a handsome plant for a sunny dry spot in even a cooler climate, but needs winter protection from severe frosts.

If you're looking for resilient pot plants to withstand drought and soaring temperatures, a primary choice is agapanthus, with its cool-coloured, shiny leaves and tall stems topped with flowers in white and many shades of blue. It looks elegant and graceful potted and demands little water. The pristine dwarf *Agapanthus* 'Snow Goose' growing in a broad band in a long planter, perhaps combined with a few wisps of common trailing ivy, is a cooling summer sight. Although traditionally regarded as tender in cool climates, European nurserymen are telling us they now have hardy varieties that I have optimistically purchased. After their first winter at West Green some remained, so more were bought, and now after several cold winters most have survived and it will be interesting to see if this favourite plant can really earn its place as a truly resilient candidate.

Even the toughest plants will dry out quickly in a pot during summer. To keep them happy, choose lighter-coloured pots rather than black or dark coloured ones, which absorb heat. Glazed pots are best as they are not porous, but if you choose pots made from concrete and terracotta it helps to paint these inside with a sealant before use to create a membrane to stop the water seeping into the pottery. Always opt for the largest pots your space will take and, in dry periods, use widely available wetting agents or water crystals to help prevent soils from drying out. Some composts are formulated with water-retentive agents – ask your compost supplier for advice. Group pots together containing plants that require the same amount of water, and water them early or late in the day when the heat is not intense. This not only means less water will evaporate but also avoids the danger of water splashing onto leaves on a hot day, which may scorch them, leaving them either brown or shrivelled. Don't place pots too close to a wall or an architectural overhang: these are known as rain-shadow areas, as pots won't benefit from any rain that nature does bring.

Pots can be messy to water, so bring the soil at least 20cm below the rim of the pot, then place small river pebbles as mulch around your planting. They look attractive, help to keep in moisture and prevent soil from spilling out. Gravel will do the same trick but as it is lighter it will spill out more easily when watering – so I prefer pebbles because they look sturdier and tidier. Water pots by hand with a hose, allowing the water to reach the rim and soak through the pot. Avoid watering with what I call a florist's mist on top as this encourages roots to come to the surface to seek the moisture and also wets the leaves, which may then burn in the sun.

Of course, after days of rain, pots will become waterlogged. To avoid this make sure the pot has adequate drainage: it should have a hole in its base and broken crocks or stones should be placed in the pot before the compost is added. If this doesn't prove adequate, try to empty out any surface water.

Drainage

Good drainage is essential not only in cool wet gardens, but also imperative in dry-climate gardens where rain, when it comes, often arrives as heavy cloudbursts. What to do with excess water is one of the garden designer's first considerations. In cool temperate gardens plants are more likely to have to cope with minor seasonal flooding through run-off from roads or sloping land, and poor neighbouring drainage.

Once the standard recommendation for improving drainage in a wet garden would have been to construct an agricultural drain consisting of a very deep trench filled with rubble dug deep into the subsoil, but current trends tell us to respect the soil's natural layers and common practice is now to construct a very narrow trench. This is filled with a single plastic geotec-covered pipe laid in a bed of gravel just deep enough – approx 1.2m – to accommodate the hole dug for the average tree, and the drain is directed to a rubble-filled pit or pond at the lowest point of a large garden, or in urban gardens into the public drainage system (with the advice of a plumber).

As a country gardener I have gently sloping pasture directing run-off into the garden. Earlier gardeners had used this run-off to create a small lake, but by the time I arrived deep gashes of erosion had appeared and deposited silt had turned the lake into a marshland inhabited by grass snakes and adders. We took many months to reform and remake the lake, but failed to solve the basic drainage problem and the area was still impassable after heavy rain. The solution was to have a parallel pair of drainage ditches dug as neat canals at right angles to the sloping field to form two drains that would feed into a nearby stream that in turn empties into the lake. These canals were designed to capture the water from the sloping pasture before it soaked into the lakeside's surrounds. I hoped the design would be both another garden feature and a demonstration of how nuisance water could be both useful as well as decorative.

This is an area known to have surplus water in winter and then it dries out in summer, so it was the perfect spot to test how well a group of plants could handle excessive water, along with exposure to cold winter winds and warm summer dryness. The ridge between the canals has been planted with *Iris sibirica*, where they thrive as they are forgiving plants that perform well in dry beds, on sloping verges and in ground

Opposite: Like a lazy serpentine, the new drainage ditches at West Gree House are crossed by five chinoiserie-inspired bridges.

that becomes a bog from time to time. With fine long leaves and superlative flowers in shades from midnight blue graduating to mauve and white, they flower in spring. *I. sibirica* 'Papillon' is an incredible sight as a mass-planted, central blue line. One of the banks has hellebores, plants that look fragile but are not. Hellebores often flower above a dusting of snow, but in warm climates they will stay green and flower provided they are given dappled shade and some water in the heat of summer. I grew *Helleborus sternii* in Australia; its leaves remind me of warm pewter and the flowers are apple-green flushed maroon. *Helleborus* x *hybridus* is pure white, flowering from late winter, and *H. argutifolius* develops into a taller plant 80cm high, with its bunches of lime green blooms lasting well into the spring, held above large, dissected, dull green leaves.

Trying to achieve undulating mounds of seasonal white groupings, I have planted spiraea, one of the most undemanding plants. *Spiraea nipponica* 'Snowmound' is covered with small bunches of white flowers among mid-green leaves as summer arrives, and *Spiraea thunbergii* gracefully arches with the finest light green leaves and masses of tiny flowers in early spring. These plants will grow along parched driveways, needing no more than a good haircut to keep their shape, and they will hedge well. *Viburnum plicatum* 'Watanabe' accompanies the spiraea, its low spreading branches carrying bracts of white flowers growing horizontally in sun or shade, and happy with occasional water. *V. plicatum* 'Mariesii' has a beautifully tiered, wedding-cake effect and looks the essence of fragility when it flowers in early summer, but it survives days of heat or heavy rain. *Hydrangea paniculata*

Below left: The dam at Kennerton Green was glamorised into a small lake by planting that included *Iris sibirica* and *Iris germanica*. A similar exercise to that at West Green House where drainage lines have been gentrified into streams by planting.

Clockwise from top left: Spiraea nipponica 'Snowmound'; *Viburnum plicatum*; *Helleborus x hybridus*; *Helleborus sternii* 'Broughton Beauty'; *Helleborus argutifolius*.

Right: A perfect planting of resilient plants – roses and lavender at the feet of *Pyrus salicifolia*.

Below: *Hydrangea quercifolia*.

'Limelight' loathed the seasonal dry shade on the canal's embankments, but *H. quercifolia* has flourished with its feet in lashings of leaf mulch.

The opposite banks of my drainage canals are being colonised by white day lilies, *Hemerocallis* 'Joan Senior', that are multiplying well and as uncomplaining here as in any dry, warm garden. Above the irises a line of graceful, silver-leafed weeping pears, *Pyrus salicifolia* var. *orientalis* 'Pendula', cast the finest shade. This is a gold-star small tree for it grew in my warm-climate garden beside a gravelled courtyard on the driest corner, and in England it grows on a shaded ridge with the water-filled drain just below and grey willows forming a cool canopy above.

I could have chosen alternative drainage solutions, such as installing a raised earth or concrete ridge to divert the flow from the fields. Or I could have made long trenches filled with gravel, covering agricultural drainage pipes to direct excess water to form a bog area, a garden feature enjoyed in many European gardens where moisture-loving plants, often of Amazonian proportions, thrive. But in warmer and drier areas, excess water is an intermittent phenomenon, so in a resilient garden plants must be found if a lush illusion of a jungle is desired that perform, whether the soil is moist or bone dry.

Bamboos grow in ditches and along roadsides in Southeast Asia, and as a cathedral vault of arched canes in the astonishing *bambouseraie* in Cevennes, southern France, but I have to admit that bamboo's attractions generally escape me. Bamboo grew in my first dry garden in Burrumbuttock, New South Wales. Our clump was very old, decorated with intermittent green leaves and cloaked with brown falling wisps, reeds and old leaves. Nobody wished to tackle the problem of clearing it, for it was known to be a refuge for reptiles, so it stood sad and neglected until one day a lethal variety of snake emerged from it to the joy of my kitten who thought it was there for a game. The kitten was saved, the bamboo removed and my liking for the plant slipped away forever.

However, bamboo is a vast genus from 6m tall giants to just thickets of leaves, which make excellent ground cover. Despite my feelings about it, some forms are undeniably garden-worthy. The graceful and arching new stems of black bamboo, *Phyllostachys nigra*, darken with age until they become dramatic columns of black, and the plant grows from the tropics into cool temperate gardens. This is said to be a non-invasive form, but whenever I've designed with bamboo I have submerged barricades of corrugated iron or some other impenetrable material around the roots. Reaching a height of 4m, the huge fast-growing arrow bamboo, *Pseudosasa japonica*, makes a hardy hedge or screen. *Pleioblastus* spp. are suitable for small gardens

and *Pleioblastus humilis* var. *pumilus* is grown as textured ground cover, achieving about 15cm in the sun and 60cm in shade, as suitable in a container as in the ground. Dwarf white-striped bamboo, *Pleioblastus variegatus*, is scarcely larger, and its green leaves have stark white variegation. Heavenly or sacred bamboo, *Nandina domestica*, is extremely adaptable, found all over the Far East and equally at home in a northern climate. Its slender canes will make an evergreen thicket about 2m tall, the new leaves emerge pinkish red and it has panicles of creamy white flowers in summer, but its greatest virtue is its crimson-flushed leaves in autumn followed by winter sprays of rich red berries. Well-fed soil and plentiful water bring out its best but it will survive drought. The dwarf form, N. 'Fire Power', is ideal for a small garden, slowly spreading into a 1m tall mat, its red-purple leaves glowing with colour all winter.

Left: *Pleiobiastus variegatus.*

Right: *Phyllostachys nigra.*

Above: Luckily, we never need to water from vintage water butts these days, but you have to admit this old equipment looks very fetching in the garden.

With long-arching evergreen leaves rising 70cm from basal clumps, the lengthy stems of the New Zealand rock lily, *Arthropodium cirratum*, flourish in warm climates in dry or well-watered surroundings, sending out a galaxy of star-like flowers. This would be a tolerant addition to any planting with a tropical feeling. I have grown it successfully beside the beach on Dangar Island and under dappled shade inland where frosts could be severe. I'm assured the dwarf form is performing well in southern England, but some shelter for the bronze-leafed dwarf *A. candidum* 'Cappucino', with its small white flowers, seems sensible.

Water conservation

Water is now a limited and expensive resource, not only for people who live in dry areas but increasingly even in temperate climates too, so it should be used economically to guarantee a continuous supply. Logical laws on the use of water would help gardeners to plant and plan more efficiently. Even in England hosepipes are often banned in summer, and in many parts of Australia local councils are encouraging everyone to install water tanks such as I grew up with, where all water held in such tanks was for household use, with plants receiving only used household water in dry spells. Some towns in the arid west of New South Wales have through necessity had two water systems, one set of pipes delivering pure drinking water, the other removing and recycling grey water to be reused for domestic gardens, toilets and the greening of the town. Domestic recycling schemes may be adopted by dry-climate gardeners everywhere as tanks can be installed internally or externally with little problem. These allow us to save, store and purify waste from the bath, washing machines and other household appliances (except toilets) to be reused for flushing toilets and watering the garden. Naturally this will be a limited source of water, but it helps.

Watering by hand

Watering must be governed by common sense. And, of course, rainwater is always the preference. Every new plant needs water to establish its root system and grow, but once it becomes obvious that all is well and the plant looks established, irrigation should be reduced so that it gradually learns to become more self-sufficient. In fact, most gardens are over-watered.

Do not water just because it is a warm day; first check with a finger or a hand tool as the earth's crust may be bone dry, even after heavy rain, but it is often moist beneath. Over-watering causes soil leaching, shallow rooting and excessive and unsustainable new growth. Your plant will tell you if it's over-watered – it will look sick, be yellowing, losing leaves, its roots will rot; in fact it becomes an unpleasant sight. The jet of water from an unregulated handheld hose can compact the soil or wash it away, and powerful jets can snap tender stems, so fix a water-breaking attachment to reduce the force and volume of delivery. Garden centres and catalogues offer many varieties – choose one that simply cuts the volume of water, then direct the water to the plants' roots and avoid any splashing back onto flowers and leaves as this not only risks scorching, but may also transmit fungal spores from the soil to the leaves.

When drought came to my Australian garden, my policy was to use what water we had for the large trees and shrubs and forget the rest. This was because the trees and shrubs had taken many decades to establish, but roses and perennials could be cut back so any moisture available could be directed to their roots rather than to new growth, and annuals are just annuals and could be planted again next year.

Your plant will tell you if it's over-watered – it will look sick, be yellowing, losing leaves, its roots will rot…

soil

It is the plants we choose that create our gardens, but the way we garden is equally important. Along with sensible use and conservation of water, soil preparation is a priority. As we are focusing on plants that will accept the widest range of temperatures across Mediterranean and cool temperate climate zones, we need to give them every assistance. Cool temperate winters can mean five to six months of cold, wet and often boggy conditions that are a complete anathema for sun-loving plants which will simply rot if their roots sit in wet soil.

There's been an increasing trend for gravel gardens in the last decade, and gravel is an excellent medium in cool climate zones for reflecting heat to warmth-loving species. However, a spread of gravel is not a quick fix for the basic problems faced by dry-climate plants in cool temperate zones during the months when low light, cold and misty rain are prolonged. All plants that love the sun will thrive more contentedly near any material that reflects warmth, but gravel on top of the soil does not address the problem of how to keep soil at the right consistency so it can hold water during the dry and provide drainage after wet periods. It will, of course, help to suppress weeds and those of us who garden in drier areas often use it as an attractive mulch to protect surface soil from excessive heat and retain moisture.

Cool temperate winters can mean five to six months of cold, wet and often boggy conditions that are a complete anathema for sun-loving plants …

Plants from the cooler zones need help where the weather is warmer than they are accustomed to, and although shade is important, soil holds the key. Always aim for a rich friable soil that will allow a good moisture balance and effective drainage. Conventional wisdom used to tell us to achieve this by first digging over the whole garden and then incorporating good compost. Another recommendation was heavy double digging right down to the subsoil, which to my mind is a lot of work to no great advantage. I would simply recommend building up to good friable soil by layering it with organic compost.

It's to our advantage to produce as much compost as possible…

Compost

All gardeners demand a lot from their soil, crowding beds with a range of plants that need nourishment to flower from early spring into winter. Compost is the natural food for all plants, providing many of the nutrients they require, and this recycled green waste makes for sustainable gardening. Think of the great trees of the forests worldwide; these are all grown on nature's recycled green waste in a constant cycle of replacement, because the nutrients the trees are extracting from the soil are returned when their leaves fall to produce compost on the forest floor. It is wise to follow nature when we can. Gardeners should try to produce as much compost as possible, but as space for compost-making in many city gardens is miniscule,

store-bought compost is a good second best. A huge range of bags is stacked high at plant centres, but some of these composts contain little or no goodness, and others may contain chemical fertilisers that can sometimes upset the balance of the elements in the soil, especially iron. Ask your gardening friends or a good nursery for recommendations as some mixes are definitely better than others, and if you add any small garden sweepings and a shovelful or two of grass clippings once in a while, this will improve the compost.

A mass of information has been written about making the perfect compost and I am always terribly impressed when I visit good gardens and see fit young men atop the steaming compost heaps, turning them to ensure the green waste rots evenly! I physically cannot do this, so I have a common-sense compost recipe for manageable green waste. It is not an exact science, but what is required is a good balance of ingredients, air and water to encourage the ideal warm moist environment for micro-organisms to proliferate and break down the material. Lime may need to be added if the soil is slightly acid. A mixture of carbon-based (dry/brown) material, such as shredded cardboard, woody stems, leaves and small twigs, and nitrogen-based (wet/green) material, including green weeds and kitchen waste, is advised. The ratio of the two should ideally be approximately 20–25 parts carbon to 1 part nitrogen, but you don't have to be too precise.

Opposite: In a Dupont garden in Maryland, USA, compost made from the waste of the vegetable patch becomes useful for growing a seasonal crop of pumpkins, before being spread out next season

Above: I feel slightly ashamed of my decomposing compost baskets, filled each year with waste from my vegetable garden, where a crop of potatoes is grown on the surface layer early in the season, then replanted with autumn annuals. The compost is used for top dressing in winter.

Larger gardens can have the ideal three-bin system – one in use on the garden, one maturing and one being filled – but there are many excellent composting bins that provide convenient and quick alternatives. Some have a central cone that pulls in air for better aeration and quicker decomposition; some rotate to make mixing easy. It is always a good idea to have two bins as it is best to fill one completely and then let the material decompose rather than trying continually to top up what you've got – this can ruin the process. Stack green waste in the bin in layers to achieve a reasonable balance. Almost all garden and household vegetable waste can be used, but only use thin layers of grass mowings or they will just become repulsive sludge. Some people prefer to compost leaves separately but I add deciduous leaves to the general mix and put evergreens through a small mulching machine before tossing them in. If it can be obtained, include occasional layers of animal manure to produce more heat and faster decomposition. If the material seems rather wet, add more dry material such as shredded paper; if it's too dry, add water – aim for just moist, not soggy.

Compost will heat up faster in a plastic bin than a wooden one and some bins promise usable compost within three months, though a year is more typical. Perhaps, use commercial accelerators that employ bacteria and enzymes to break down vegetable and cellulose-type waste and speed composting, but if I can grow a vegetative accelerator this is the best. Comfrey, *Symphytum officinale*, is a top-rated accelerator: place leaves between layers of green wastes but do not add roots or you'll end up with a comfrey heap. Yarrow, *Achillea millefolium*, is another good candidate and both flowers and foliage can be added. I have used commercial accelerators in the past, but now, having yarrow growing I do not bother. *A. millefolium* is one of the most resilient plants I know and its colour range is exceptional, so a patch in the garden is a win-win situation.

Animal manure speeds up microbial action to help decomposition. Adding animal manures to garden beds provides the same action, helping plants to absorb soil nutrients. Farmers do still sell bagged manure, but this is not the easiest component to bring home in the family car – I will never forget the end of a family picnic beside the Mitta Mitta River, when my father, reaching for the newspaper to wrap the fire irons and tea billy, found Mother had already appropriated it for dried cowpats, placed carefully between the folds! All fresh manures must be put aside for at least three to six months to decompose as fresh manure contains lots of urine (ammonia). I would generally recommend adding a spadeful or two of manure to the composting mixture rather than using it straight. Don't overdo the manure in a garden full of dry-climate, resilient plants as many do not like soils too rich; for them I mix instead a spadeful of gravel with my compost to assist with drainage.

Big roots, branches and end-of-season perennials can be chipped by contractors or local council machines, or if fires aren't banned burn them for ash, which is an excellent potash-rich soil additive. In fact, a bonfire is also the spot for pernicious weeds whose seeds could infect a compost. Although chipped material doesn't contain many nutrients, it is good top mulch and lurking seeds will not germinate in it in the first year. It can be added to improve soil structure or mixed into compost heaps. Domestic chipping machines are for me a story on their own. The first one I purchased was terrifying to feed but would devour only the lightest material. A stouter model was obtained which ate a little more accompanied by decibels of noise and still left the problem of perennial roots and tough sticks, so finally I called in a contractor to do the shredding.

Left: Achillea millefolium is not only a superb resilient plant, it also is one of the best vegetative accelerators for a compost heap.

Mulching and fertilising

Mulching conserves moisture in the soil, discourages weed growth and protects plant roots from scorching sun or freezing frost. A generous mulch of garden compost also adds fertility as organisms in the soil break it down and take it into the soil. Every gardener I know has definite opinions about the best ways to mulch. Some are much more desirable than others. Tiny Dangar Island lies midstream towards the mouth of the Hawkesbury River north of Sydney. The island is reached by ferry and the houses by a path across the island from the wharf. My neighbours were a relaxed family, definitely not gardeners, who perhaps would one weekend a month put the old Victa mower over the more-than-verdant grass. As I arrived at my gate one Friday afternoon I casually looked across my yard and was stunned to see the whole of the neighbours' backyard cleared and immaculately dug over, with tiny plants evenly spaced out in regimented rows. But what stopped me in my tracks was the compost: the whole garden had been covered with a several-inches-thick layer of the *Sydney Morning Herald*. It looked horrendous. In the twilight I stared hard at these sturdy seedlings composted so carefully with newspaper. When I first looked I thought them tomatoes, but I peered again and realised – I was looking at a quarter acre of marijuana! How successful the compost was I do not know, for by the next weekend the parents came home and the plants departed.

Ideally mulches should add organic matter to the soil and increase microbial activity for healthy plant growth, but however much we wish to pamper a plant, a garden is a place of beauty, so aesthetics must be considered too. Fundamentalist gardeners may advocate tufts of straw, chipped cardboard and untidy kitchen refuse as mulch, but for me it rather negates the point of gardening. Some of the popular commercial mulches are equally unsatisfactory for other reasons – chipped pine bark and nuggets are particular culprits for they draw nitrogen from the

soil in the process of decomposition and hence from the plants, causing chlorosis. Good, dark chocolaty mulch always looks wholesome when it is spread after the plants are cut back and the bed tidied at winter's end, with a further helping put around plants as spring arrives, applied when the soil is moist, not over-dry. A scattering of slow-release pellet fertiliser onto beds and containers just before spring flowering will also support the plants. Never fertilise as hot weather begins as the resulting masses of lush new growth require abundant moisture and new growth is susceptible to scorching or burning.

In cooler climates, mulch is a blanket against frost and snow damage. This winter I marvelled at a roadside planting in Vienna, which was covered with branches of fir, layer upon layer, I guess to keep the spring bulbs snug, and it looked pleasing too.

Good, dark chocolaty mulch always looks wholesome when it is spread after the plants are cut back ...

Below: A coating of disintegrating straw reduces the suns rays and helps eliminate weeds in this herb garden in central Victoria.

Opposite: Good, rich compost looking like the best chocolate, makes the ideal mulch; an added bonus is that it's darkness is a perfect foil for the plants above.

soil types

Gravel and sand

There is very little nourishment in soils that are primarily gravel and sand. They are formed by the weathering of rocks and are porous – any nutrients or water that pass through them do so very quickly, over-draining, leaving very few if any benefits behind, which leads to dehydration and problems in retaining moisture and nutrients. These soils need copious nourishment with mulch applied at least twice a year in spring and before winter. Then I would add blood and bonemeal, broadly casting it onto lawn and beds alike, around six weeks before the first flush of flowers. If a new plant likes a rich soil, it should be planted with mulch as well.

Clay

When digging over a garden patch, you will often find a clod of lumpy, solid soil coloured grey-blue like a lump of Plasticine comes up. Clay soils are made up of fine particles, leaving few air spaces, so drainage is extremely poor, causing plants in time of rains to become waterlogged. Red clay soils are not as dense and, although they suffer many of the same problems, they have more nutrients and drain a little better.

Loam

This is the soil we all dream about gardening on. Friable and easy to dig, it is made up of 40 per cent sand, 40 per cent silt and 20 per cent clay and is full of organic matter and is nutrient rich. However, in hot weather even rich soils dry out and need water, but here the water will penetrate gently to the plants' roots and be absorbed.

Peat

Peat contains more organic matter than other soils and its acidity inhibits the decomposition process. It also tends to have fewer nutrients than other soils and is prone to retain water. However, peat, with care and good management, fertilisers and drainage, responds well.

Chalk

A good layer of top soil can help to negate some of the problems of chalk soil, for the garden is growing on stony and alkaline soil that blocks the trace elements, such as iron and magnesium, which inhibits growth. Chalk soil dries out quickly and, as it is of poor quality, needs a regular supply of mulch and fertilisers.

Coastal

Coastal soils tend to be both sandy and alkaline with the characteristics of both these soil types. They often contain brackish water in the subsoil because coastal areas have been continuously subjected to salt and erosion through storms, tides and wind. Many plants simply do not like salt – either it burns their leaves or their roots are troubled. Deep mulching can make the soil less alkaline, but salt always rises through the soil through watering, making plant selection paramount.

Clay soils

Clay soils present severe drainage problems, and are particularly problematic for plants that prefer dry conditions. Clay is a very dense soil and the particles bind together when wet to form watertight basins, then when it is hot it is rock hard, cracks and is nearly impossible to dig. In other words, it forms a facsimile of a clay pot. For the best chance of success when planting in clay soils, dig huge holes about double the size of the canopy of the plant, adding compost and coarse sand or gravel – but use only thoroughly well-rotted material as manure or the like develops enormous heat as it breaks down, burns roots and sets plants back if it does not kill them. I have been advised to install drainage lines to the base of planting holes in serious clay to remove excess water, but so far it has never been necessary. Clay soils should be prepared by digging them over thoroughly, incorporating compost and aerating materials before planting, but I am often too impatient and can't wait to start, so my new beds tend to resemble volcanic craters.

Right: Clay soils can look unsightly, cracked and arid during dry periods.

Drainage

Sometimes extreme solutions may be required. I had great difficulty stopping a row of three espaliered plum trees in the vegetable garden at Kennerton Green from rotting from even normal watering. Although drainage pipes had been installed in the garden, after long periods of rain extra ground and surface water collected naturally beside the edge of the path where they were planted. To overcome this problem the trees were lifted from their position at ground level, then a small timber frame 100 x 100 x 120cm high was placed above each vacated hole. The bottom of each hole was filled with rubble and good compost was placed on top, so when the trees were replanted they were now being put into raised beds, lifting the roots above the underground water and providing the extra drainage they needed to survive. Exactly the same problem occurred to a row of yews at West Green House, but once they were lifted above the water table in exactly the same manner, they thrived and now the hedge is immaculate.

Above: A simple drain has been dug to lay an irrigation pipe.

Below left and right: Gravel will assist with drainage also, however the main drain is the agricultural pipe.

Planting a tree

One of the keys to the satisfactory growth of trees and shrubs is the preparation of the planting hole. For even small trees, a hole may be 1m across and for more mature trees allow a width of twice the existing branch span and depth at least double the specimen's root length. Cover the base of the hole with rubble for drainage and then fill the entire cavity with water. As it subsides, place the seedling tree in the hole so that it will be planted with its trunk at the same soil depth as the level in the container, and place a length of plastic pipe diagonally towards the roots of the tree with its top end just above the surface of the planting hole. Fill the hole with good compost, firming it in by hand with more earth, and water again very slowly until the surface is quite wet. Then finally install a protective tree guard. Fill the pipe with water at weekly intervals during dry periods, so that the water is slowly absorbed by the roots.

it was inevitable that a little plant knowledge
would come my way by osmosis…

green structure

Growing up with a garden-obsessed mother and grandmother who had both created inland Australian gardens, it was inevitable that a little plant knowledge would come my way by osmosis, but when I acquired one of New South Wales' very serious cool temperate gardens I realised I needed to know much more. So a partner and I invited knowledgeable gardeners whom we considered garden gurus from the UK, Europe and the USA to Australia to lecture in what developed into the Australia-wide Garden Lecture series.

This became quite an exercise, for up to six weeks annually over ten years I drove our guests thousands of miles, listening to their lectures over and over again, in auditoriums that ranged from old private ballrooms in once-isolated homesteads to dusty sheds. Our lecturers taught us garden design, history, plant groupings and colour and adjusted their lectures to the local climate zone in our lecture circuit. This covered a range from almost alpine conditions, through cool temperate and Mediterranean climates to the hard landscapes that verged on desert. But one lecturer never changed her subject matter, as she spoke of the garden's skeleton, the trees, hedges, avenues, small

copses and shapes that hold a planting design together. She had selected a collection of green plants in many shades and textures that can not only serve to support and enhance a more floriferous planting, but on their own can make a delightfully smart garden that will grow in the widest climate range.

Her chosen plants were ones even the ancient civilisations knew to be hardy. By 100BC the Roman Pliny the Younger was writing in his letters that he cut his box, *Buxus sempervirens*, into 'a thousand shapes' next to walls of cyprus, *Cupressus*, and ivy, *Hedera* spp. From the wall paintings preserved at Pompeii, in medieval manuscripts and baroque European parterres, box etches much of the history of gardening. Wherever we look, from cool northern countries to the shores of the Mediterranean, from the southern USA's humid gardens to dusty inland spaces, box will flourish with nothing more than a weekly watering in the height of summer. It is slow to propagate and takes a good year for reasonable roots to form, but when it has established a rooting system it may be planted out into any well-composted and reasonably drained soil, and once *in situ* it establishes quickly to become among the most accommodating of green plants. In warm climates it does like a deep soaking, and in any climate give it plant food in spring and summer, but otherwise it gets by with occasional watering.

Planted in pots, perhaps clipped into a range of shapes and sizes, box plants can form a grouping that can be trimmed to be extremely elegant or can add sustainable quirkiness – the fun a garden often needs. Imaginative use of box as green structure can be translated to a garden of any size in a wide range of climates. Box never seems to go out of fashion, and features regularly in prizewinning gardens at England's Chelsea Flower Show. Recently British designer Tom Stewart Smith placed large clipped balls of *Buxus sempervirens* to form substantial rows of what resembled dense, green bouncy balls as a boundary divide. In a

Opposite: The weaving of precisely clipped cushions of *Buxus* surrounded by the informality of grasses make us understand why the Jardin du Plume in Normandy is regarded as one of the most exciting modern gardens in Europe.

Above: In a new English garden geometric mounds of green, using box and grasses, create modernistic cubes that make excellent resilient planting.

Below: A fine example of a traditional green European parterre that showcases green design.

previous year Swedish designer Ulf Nordfjell installed a garden of ordered perennials in drifts among fine young birch, the soft meadow-like effect anchored with solid, deep green plants, including box cut into round shapes. The design was a tribute to the Swedish botanist Linnaeus, using plants and materials suitable for their country and at the show's end it was transplanted to flourish in southern Sweden.

In Brittany, in a garden close to the sea, box has been trained up apple trees to resemble serpents, and in my garden it forms the Queen of Hearts, originally trained to wires with the solid shape formed by regular clipping. In summer, its growth is vigorous but shapes will stay sharp if clipped once the frosts are gone, needing no more than a gentle tidy before frosts return. My 2m tall 'Queen' took approximately eight years to become the required shape, starting from a 30cm plant placed at the base of a wire frame, made for me by a firm I saw advertising this service.

Unfortunately there is one serious drawback with box in cool temperate climates. Box blight strips leaves away to twiggy growth and unsightly bare patches, and plants have to be dug up and destroyed. The disease is caused by two fungi, *Cylindro-cladium buxicola* and *Volutella buxi*, and has devastated commercial stocks and private gardens alike over the last two decades throughout much of Europe. Symptoms begin with spots on the leaves and black streaks on the stems and branches, often with patches of greyish fungus on the lower leaf surface, but most gardeners notice the disease only once the leaves begin to disappear and reveal the twiggy growth. If plants are affected, they will not recover and cannot be replanted as the spores stay in the ground, so alternatives have to be found. Gardeners in hot climates won't be troubled by the disease as the spores cannot survive hot dry summers where the temperature rises above 33°C (91°F).

Opposite: The gardens of Le Grand Launay in Brittany are sculptures of green. Here serpents twist up apple trees and wind sinuously across the lawn.

Below left: A colonial garden outlined in traditional green structure.

Below right: Box used in a classical style that is striking and timeless.

Resilient alternatives to box

Fortunately there are other tolerant hedging plants
with small leaves suitable for clipping, including
many berberis forms with good foliage and flowers
or berries, their one disadvantage being that some are
very spiny. *Berberis buxifolia* 'Pygmaea' will tolerate any
well-drained soil, it is fully drought-resistant and will
stand cold exposed locations. B. *stenophylla* 'Irwinii' has
attractive yellow flowers, and B. *thunbergii* 'Atropurpurea
Nana' is a good compact purple-leafed form. *Ilex crenata*,
Japanese or box-leafed holly, forms an excellent low
hedge with leaves rather similar to box and small,
black, shiny fruits in winter. After the emotional
devastation of having to throw away many thousands
of defoliating box plants at West Green, I tried dwarf
Ilex dimorphophylla 'Somerset Pixie' as a substitute to
outline beds or parterres. It was rather patchy to
establish, but once it was happy the small, deep green
leaves and attractive red winter berries became a viable
alternative. It clips well and does not grow rampantly.
Any evergreen holly will be hardy and accept virtually
all soils and either sun or shade, needing just sensible
amounts of water during dry spells. Yew, *Taxus baccata*,
is another possible deep green substitute, but it is
best clipped at heights above 1m so is not suitable for
low designs, and it's really for the cooler garden.

The fine-leafed, dense green *Lonicera nitida* is perhaps
the commonest substitute in gardens that have been
devastated by box blight. It grows quickly, it is happy
in virtually any situation, it can be clipped neatly
into hedges and is easily trainable into any shape, but
its disadvantage is its speed of growth. I used it for
topiary in my garden at Kennerton Green where it
relished the warmth and grew outrageously, needing a
weekly clipping – and even in colder Europe it requires
vigilance and needs clipping once a month or so. On
the plus side, it is undemanding, it will thrive in cold,
snow, or in a concrete pot in a hot climate, so it must
find a place among resilient structural plants.

*Opposite: Lonicera nitida can also make
the most precise hedges. Here
it frames a firework burst of the
bare-coloured branches of Cornus
in winter.*

Opposite top right: Ilex crenata.

*Opposite bottom right: Berberis
thunbergii.*

Fortunately
there are
other tolerant
hedging plants,
including
many berberis
forms... .

Right and far right: Some gardens absolutely stop you in your tracks, and the design originality at Crech Pape comes in this category. Here green structure has been used to create the story of the garden, which is both glamorous and witty.

Clipped and natural shapes

Careful plant selection will dictate the feel of a garden. At the garden of Crech Pape, overlooking the coast of Brittany, I found a spectacular twenty-year-old garden where the selection of resilient plants and pattern of planting created an instant sense of rhythm. Sand dunes and the Atlantic Ocean are almost touchable from this garden and the temperature ranges from the 30°Cs in summer to just below zero in winter. This district can grow a smorgasbord of plants where the widest range of species live in juxtaposition; desert aloes and *Agave americana* can grow alongside rainforest dicksonias and temperate flowering prunus and magnolias, so it takes a sure hand to limit the choice.

The lower garden is designed in a series of ascending circles, partly formed through hard landscaping where the circular beds rise up from a sunken central point, with the shape of its plants reinforcing the curving pattern. Clipped balls of small-leafed plants make solid structures with soft, floating mounds of golden *Hakonechloa macra* 'Aureola' placed at regular intervals to create a planting tempo. *Hakonechloa* are truly beautiful, arching grasses; green, yellow and golden varieties all form gracefully soft but dense round shapes with long, curving stems, and they are happy in full sun or dappled shade. Given reasonable water, the grasses grow to 35cm and provide adaptable structural forms. In this French garden at the time of my visit in mid-autumn their soft, bosomy curves were highlighted by seasonal colour – the copper-leafed *Dahlia* 'Bishop of Llandaff' with its single scarlet flowers, golden crocosmia and tawny kniphofia all towered above the grass shapes. Although to me they seemed almost superfluous, they did help to emphasise how well the mass of solid green forms looked.

Careful plant selection will dictate the feel of a garden

Trees can not only make a garden's structure but also dictate its mood through their shape…

We know that trees can not only make a garden's structure but also dictate its mood through their shape, colour and leaf texture. The easiest subjects for clipping are trees and shrubs with dense compact foliage of small leaves or needles, but even vast trees such as the Scots pine, *Pinus sylvestris*, can be clipped and trained when young to make impressive small trees. Large-leafed and deciduous trees can also be clipped and the Japanese technique of clipping large shrubs into curved shapes to resemble rolling clouds is intriguing. These green sculptures can be a very convenient way of transforming out-of-control old bushes into attractive forms or clipped into the delicate 'cloud trees' that

give Oriental gardens their unique charm. One of the most impervious plants I've ever grown (and more often grubbed out) has been *Abelia* x *grandiflora*. It is a good bushy shrub, with deep green to bronze leaves, it's evergreen in warmer climates, becoming more deciduous in cooler lands, and hardy to just below freezing with tube-like bell flowers in gentle pink. This plant was a firm favourite in the old gardens I knew, but usually appeared only as uncontrolled, rather dusty-coloured lumps – it would have been an excellent candidate for clipping into a cloud formation to give it purpose. Recently I saw the most striking collection of clipped cubes, dense squares of

cerise-pink bells and was amazed to realise it was *Abelia* x *floribunda*. Well clipped, it made a powerful statement, but when the bush is left alone it is rather nondescript. At West Green House, I purchased already mature and clipped cloud trees made from oversized plants of *Lonicera nitida*. The shapes are created by cutting away all but a few well-positioned branches, which are then partly stripped to leave small branches at specific intervals where the leaves are clipped to resemble small, green clouds.

The forbearing ivy is often regarded as a curse, but it is extremely tough and resilient and will happily accept being clipped and trained into ornamental shapes, along garlands or over decorative frames. Kept clipped and under control, it covers unsightly fences and walls and makes a shiny green backdrop to a garden.

One of the most extreme examples of clipped structure must be the green maze. I'm not sure whether a maze should rate as a tantalising green concept or a warped mind's idea of green fun, but however a maze is perceived it can certainly provide a monumental green structure, generally constructed either of yew in northern Europe or of cypresses in warmer parts.

Above left: Common ivy clips into elegant green shapes.

Above right: Bushes of *Abelia* x *grandiflora* are stalwarts of old gardens, and so often grubbed out and discarded, but clipped into either cloud shapes or precise geometric forms, it can make garden architecture.

green structure

Landforms

There are moments in a gardening life that are pure exhilaration, and I have always been excited by gardens where the structure is created through predominantly green shapes and plants. As a novice gardener, I was over-awed by the great green box parterre at Villandry in France. Then came the green landforms of Emma Keswick and Charles Jencks' garden in Scotland where 17 acres (6.8 hectares) had been fashioned into an extraordinary landscape of vast sculpted earthworks, reflective lakes and engineered structures. This is design and structure on a scale nearly unknown in this century's domestic landscapes, and questions many garden design fundamentals. Jencks' garden shows that a resilient garden can have different aspirations and inspiring gardens can be determined entirely by

Below: At Scampston Hall in Yorkshire, garden designer Piet Oudolf has created green sculpture forming a mount as an architectural feature – a bold green centrepiece in a design supported by alleys of pleach trees and beds of interwoven grasses and perennials.

Opposite top: Charles Jencks' landscape design, using just green form and water at the Scottish National Gallery.

Opposite bottom: Kim Wilkie's green masterpiece at Boughton Park in Northamptonshire.

structure rather than plant content. The Jencks gardens, like the one he designed for the Gallery of Modern Art in Edinburgh, are covered in turf which is suitable for a construction on the cool edge of the cool temperate climate, but I have seen mounds formed to look like mini ziggurats covered in rougher local grasses, so the covering of dramatic earth shapes can be adjusted to suit the climate.

I was similarly humbled when I came across an earthwork in the classical landscape of Boughton Park in Northamptonshire, England. The rim of this work is invisible until you approach it and realise you are standing at the edge of a 70m square, looking into a pyramid descending 7m into the earth with a grass path at its side, which leads a visitor down

to a rectangular water basin below, reflecting the blue sky above. I found the scale and concept of this giant earthwork both overwhelming and exceptional. Designed by one of garden architecture's original thinkers, Kim Wilkie, this land sculpture is a modern interpretation of a Greek legend, based on the tale of Orpheus going down into Hades to bring back his wife. As a practical gardener, I always question the maintenance of grass on steep slopes, so I was fascinated by how this masterpiece was maintained, and I was told it was mown by a remote-controlled bank mower. In more domestic-sized landscapes the worthy strimmer still manages most embankments well, so earthworks need not be ruled out; they don't have to boast enormous dimensions to make a statement.

In Northern Ireland, Mary Reynolds dipped into Irish culture for her landform interpretation of a calming landscape designed for a local spa. This is a landscape of gentle movement with low circles of slightly mounded earth outlining gravel paths to form Celtic circles, then with lawns moulded into gentle waves covered in rough grass to make rolling curves. At its perimeter, climatically suitable groups of sedges and grasses echo the earthform's movement. The planting suggested the motion of the undulating lawns that in turn reflected the rolling green landscape of Ireland beyond the garden, bringing the borrowed landscape into the picture.

Some American designers have for many years sidelined plants and created gardens principally from hard materials. I can remember the sensation caused by Martha Schwartz when she placed a grid of purple bagels over her suburban lawn, then her pond design decorated with plastic green frogs, and her serene courtyard of raked gravel dissected with just a few trees and a grid of rills in a desert garden. Her work is minimalistic and geometric, her palette restricted. The approach of designers such as these gives us new guidance for alternative garden solutions. I believe that landform designs offer exciting possibilities for structural design in any climate as they can be covered in all kinds of grasses or groundcovering plants, or clad in harder materials.

Far left: The imagery of Ireland's celtic past is woven into the green circles of this garden by Mary Reynolds, near Enniscorthy, Eire.

Left: One of modern garden design's iconic concepts – Martha Schwartz's bagel garden.

Her work is minimalistic and geometric, her palette restricted.

Right: Master plantsman Piet Oudolf uses tenacious late-flowering perennials that include erygynum and echinacea in this border at the RHS garden at Wisley.

Opposite: Using many of the same perennials with *Sedum spectabile* 'Meteor' in the foreground, Australian David Glenn creates a similar border in the vastly different climate of central Victoria, Australia. The planting also includes *Limonium peregrinum*, *Caryopteris* 'Heavenly Blue' and *Euphorbia stygiana*

plant groupings

When planning a garden it is essential to place together plants that have similar requirements for water, light, drainage or protection. In dry climates, this is often referred to as planting in water zones. This is common sense both for the health of the plant and for efficient irrigation as the installation of irrigation pipes is expensive and the visual appeal of long stretches of hoses criss-crossing a garden limited. I try to plan a garden with the most resilient plants at its perimeter, those that in their first year can survive with just a weekly watering, in a garden bed as similar as possible to the plants' natural environment, so eventually they can be ignored.

The best time to plant is in the autumn. In cooler climates, autumn's still-warm earth allows roots to settle before the harsh weather, giving them a chance to get established to perform well the following year. In warmer, drier climates, winter rains will give the roots time to develop before the stress of summer heat.

I try to plan a garden with the most resilient plants at its perimeter…

Banish any thought that plants for tough conditions are just a dull collection of morbid plants...

The success of any garden depends on the choice of plants rather than on the climatic conditions of the garden. For example, those of us who have gardened in dry climates have believed for too long that success depends on water, tempting us to plant cool-climate plants that will flower and flourish in a year of good rain but struggle without it, and leading us to cosset plants that originated in harsher climates which in fact perform just as well if not better in the austere conditions in which they were bred.

Banish any thought that plants for tough conditions are just a dull collection of morbid specimens with small grey or waxy leaves that nature developed to assist them to survive intractable positions. Many of these plants are graceful, with beautiful colour, others are grown for smart and assured garden style, and some give the garden attitude. Often, tough plants have flamboyant flowering periods, and the more we get to know them, the less likely we are to be bewitched by all those plants suitable for protected, cool temperate gardens that make us stray in nurseries. There is a wide range of plants to satisfy every garden mood without requiring either an early-morning watering as the heat rises or a frantic dash for frost covering as temperature falls.

Whatever the climate, planting a perimeter grouping depends on what lies beyond, the space available, the prevailing wind or even the urban noise. Where space is a concern, tight hedging can give a feeling of protection and privacy, it can obliterate an unwelcome view and even help as a practical wind and dust barrier. If the planting is close to other people, good manners suggest the choice of human-friendly species without lethal thorns and avoid leaves and berries that could be poisonous or toxic, although I'm not averse to leaving the odd thorn!

When hedging plants are the background, or crafted into sharp forms in their own right, their shapes and colour can set the stage for the garden's action. In cool temperate gardens yew, *Taxus baccata*, is a common formal choice and in drier gardens many varieties of cypress, *Cupressus*, will provide solid green forms. Cypresses need water only while they're getting established, then grow quickly to give tight green protection. *Cupressus macrocarpa* will grow to 25m, but it's shallow-rooted so arguably best used for high hedging and its deep yew-green evergreen foliage clips well. *C. torulosa* is a lighter green with agreeable dry-climate behaviour; it is efficient, but in recent years has been used excessively as the tree of choice for dense green windbreaks spreading mile after mile along boundaries in dry, warm areas of southern Australia, and again in new coastal developments along the Mediterranean.

I feel that where the native vegetation is grey, this tree can look incongruous and quite unharmonious. Of course, all gardening is down to personal taste, but it seems more pleasing to harmonise a boundary planting into the landscape. Grey-green is the native vegetation colour in the dry climate lands of the Mediterranean and Australia and this natural flora tone is less strident against a dry landscape. Similarly, grey-green eucalyptus looks out of place to me in a lush, green, north European landscape, not only because of its colour but also its shape. If eucalyptus trees are well watered in a cool climate, they grow lanky, like adolescents, and their leaves become tufts incongruously spaced along over-long, lax branches.

Opposite: The most resilient green structure *Cupressus macrocarpa* and *turolosa* is used to create green hedging for the rose garden at Kennerton Green.

plant
groupings

Some plants seem to harmonise better with a wider range of environments. I've often felt that exotic, fine, slender deciduous trees seem to fuse a traditional European garden to the native vegetation more successfully. Tall and slender, its fine branches covered with small, nondescript, green leaves, the amelanchier, *Amelanchier lamarckii*, has all the virtues of a front-line resilient tree. Modest in stature, it filters light and vision but does not cast dense shade. Its spring blossom is remarkable, not as flamboyant as that of the Japanese cherry, but delicate, palest pink, scented bells borne in ethereal masses. Amelanchiers grew for me in Australia in pure clay and nearly hill-top drainage with 19m mature *Pinus radiata* behind at one end, and *Cupressus turolosa* on the other, facing unbroken westerly winds, some snow, frost and weeks of hot spells (although with water once a week when it got really tough). Today, they grow at West Green House facing the winds from the open fields, their feet in poorly drained soil. I would choose a few of these blossoming trees for a resilient mini grove at the entrance to any resilient garden. To emphasise their graceful beauty, an

under-planting of arching 70cm bridal wreath, *Francoa ramosa*, with its snow-white flowers in late summer and mounded green foliage, would complement the informality of the tree, and its flower colour. In drier climates, bridal wreath must have this shade, but in milder climates it is happy with either sun or dappled shade – as tolerant as the remarkable amelanchier.

Wherever the garden, plants can be used to create contrasting moods. The versatile and tough hawthorn, *Crataegus prunifolia*, for example, can make a hedge or be clipped to form a long trunk with its deep green leaves cut to a shape you wish. As a standard it will create garden architecture; a row planted as an avenue makes a group of informal pompom trees with white blossom in spring and red autumn berries. There would be shade beneath that could be used for a bugle *Ajuga* spp., a plant impervious to shade. I would favour *Ajuga reptans* 'Catlins Giant' that spreads into a 50cm dense mat, its bronze leaves a rich foil for its 35cm-tall spires of vibrant violet flowers.

From bottom left to right: Ajuga 'Catlins Giant'; Crataegus prunifolia; Pinus radiata; Amelanchier lamarkii.

plant groupings

Resilient borders

Coming from a harsh climate, I have always and, perhaps not wisely, skirted away from the tough impervious plants recommended for hot temperatures and searched for the softer look. I always wanted a garden on my parched gravel ridge to be one billowing with drifts of flowers in demure blues, mauves, creams and pinks – all the fantasy colours of the English borders. So desperate was I when young, I emptied nurseries of every plant the revered English gardeners' books suggested for cool temperate gardens, but however hard I tried in my hot, dry climate, they were doomed to die.

Years later, I walked on a midsummer day in drought-stricken central Victoria, with the temperature hovering around 36°C (96°F), through the gardens of Australian plantsman David Glenn. Here was a vast collection of plants known worldwide from good cool temperate catalogues, but despite the searing heat they were fresh and vibrant. By planting species whose natural habitats are less than hospitable, David Glenn was the first to show me how it is possible to grow the most triumphant herbaceous border from spring into winter in a climate with rainfall of 28–50cm without supplementary watering. His plants were those versatile staples of any picture-book north European garden and now so in vogue with garden designers, painted among the fashionable grasses. In David's garden, surrounded by a 1.8m-high laurel hedge, herbaceous plants swamped two long beds that had been dug as drifts in gravelly garden soil, now coated with a fine organic mulch. These borders, as in all gardens that are carefully tended, are weeded and deadheaded and plants thinned or cut back as required, but they are not watered. They receive only an inland rainfall similar to what could be expected in Alice Springs, Mildura or Wagga Wagga, the harshest of conditions. Los Angeles receives about the same rainfall and is regarded as a desert climate.

Left: The irridescent purple of the *Salvia nemorosa* ssp. *tesquicola* in the foreground is highlighted by the blue of *Perovskia* 'Blue Spires' and the pink of *Sedum* 'Matrona' in this dry Australian garden.

Right: *Acanthus* was immortalised by ancient Greek architects. I grow it at West Green House and it makes a supreme architectural statement in David Glenn's Victorian garden, so it must be a top class resilient plant. *Allium giganteum, Salvia nemorosa* 'Lambley Dumble', *Achillea* 'Coronation Gold', *Acanthus mollis* 'Bendigo Towers'.

Left: The *Salvia* in the foreground is a form of *Salvia scarea* collected in the Taurus Mountains, Turkey. The light green foliage with white flowers is a billy button form of feverfew, *Tanacetum parthenium.*

Many expected plants were there, tough Mediteranean lavenders and rosemary, santolina and sedums in many forms. *Sedum erythrostictum* 'Frosty Morn', with its white variegated leaves and palest pink flowers, was cut back to 30cm in late spring to make it sturdier and less brittle. *S. telephium ruprechtii* 'Beth Chatto Form' was a drought-tolerant mound of blue-brushed magenta leaves above heads of knobbly, cream flowers. Euphorbias were much in evidence – *Euphorbia characias* 'Sierra Nevada', with black-eyed flower heads, and *E.* x *martini* 'Slow Life', with crimson red tips above flowers of lime. In this tough climate they did not grow as lax as in Europe, but kept a better shape as they were in the environment they came from. There were mounds of daisies too. Tansy, *Tanacetum corymbosum*, will repeat flower from spring onwards if trimmed after its first flush. The Moroccan daisy, *Rhodathemum gayanum* 'Flamingo', with its pink petals and brown eyes above blue-green foliage, frothed through the beds, and *Erigeron glaucus* 'Sea Breeze' formed a path-side hummock of pink petals around lemon centres. Another path-side daisy was *Anthemis* 'Susanna Mitchell', a creamy flower growing to about 35cm above leaves of grey-green.

However, it was the salvias that astounded me – brilliant vertical accents in blues, purples and pinks – all unwatered. These were the same varieties I grow in my English garden, where they are pampered and watered and nowhere near as luxuriant. *Salvia* x *sylvestris* 'Blauhügel' will flower for over 20 weeks in a dry, warm area if the mauve-blue spire is cut back after first flowering and then again in winter. *S. nemorosa* 'Lubecca' is treated the same way, its 30cm spikes flowering in spring and autumn. *S. fruticosa* 'Blue Ship' is 80cm of dense, mauve flower spikes, and I swear that luminous paint was bred into *S. nemorosa* 'Ostfriesland' as it simply glows purple-blue! It flowers quite early in spring and, cut sharply back, will return for a further display within weeks. The *Salvia* x *sylvestris* group performs the same way. From the back of the border growing as a shrub was blackcurrant sage, *S. microphylla* 'Margaret Arnold', up to 1.5m tall, with scattered red-pink flowers, while the spires of *S. leucantha* 'Pink Velour' were 1m bracts of soft fur. The blinding-red 60cm-high shrub *S. greggii* 'Heatwave Blaze' was covered in flowers.

Above: Sedum 'Autumn Joy', white agapanthus, perovskia and salvias growing in front of wheat silos in central Victoria looking just as fresh and vibrant as they do in a north European garden.

Top left: Linaria purpurea 'Canon Went' will overtake a garden if there is too much good food and moisture, as it has here at West Green House. It was much more controllable in a harsher garden.

Bottom right: Santolina and *Salvia officinalis* 'Purpurascens' creep onto a pathway in this garden; both Mediterranean plants are impervious to a wide climate range.

Bottom left: Olive tree with apricot-orange *Agastache aurantiaca* and silver white *Senecio viravira* in the dry garden at Lambley, Victoria.

plant groupings

In the UK, I also use the culinary salvias *S. officinalis* and *Salvia officinalis* 'Purpurascens' as edging plants and they conform to be nearly as precise as any clipped hedge. I like them mixed with the silver-white leaves of *Senecio viravira* with its lemon-butter blooms, and the 90cm-tall blue drumsticks of *Echinops ritro* subsp. *ruthenicus* – a diva that can become rampant if it sees too much water. I also like drifts of agastache in blue, mauve, pink, apricot and white, plants that can be kept under control only where water is in short supply.

David Glenn's remarkable garden is a masterclass in plant selection – those plants that enthralled me are available in good catalogues in northern Europe, America, South Africa, New Zealand and Australia, ultimately plants for a wide climate range that are reliable.

Mediterranean aromatic plants delight in this company and all these plants are good companions for a rigorously enforced no-water policy. Many will also withstand cold and frost, although the more exotic varieties of salvias are tender and need winter protection in a cold climate. Daisies, tougher salvias and many of the herbs are good neighbours with bulbs native to harsh climates and gravelly soils – allium, eremurus, lily varieties, gladioli and irises – to provide a virtuoso display from spring until the early winter frosts. Bulbs are wonderfully resilient plants as they store their nutrients and water and then disappear in order to survive until their next cycle.

And so my garden grouping of plants moves from informal, small tree groups to more architecturally formed trees, then on to beds of seasonal flowers, all including plants with a track record of reliability – these are all possible choices with just practical care in a planting that must be resilient.

Allium, eremurus, lily varieties, gladioli and irises provide a virtuoso display from spring until the early winter frosts.

Right: A Mediterranean garden in spring with bursts of purple alliums against a green background. Alliums are amongst the most forgiving of bulbs; as long as there is good drainage, they multiply quickly, looking at their best growing through dense foliage, so masking their unfortunate leaves.

Fruit trees

Gardens for me should always include fruit trees, for their beauty, their fruit and often for shelter. Although few are universally resilient, if I had the problems of limited space and limited water I'd opt to care for a tolerant fruit tree before all others. Throughout the Mediterranean countries, many houses and yards are shaded by a single fruit tree, the shade often flickering over precise lines of vegetables. The apple (Malus spp.) is not associated with warm lands, but it is one of the most forgiving of trees, fruiting even when water is intermittent or the season is dull and wet. Apples are very accommdating and can be included in gardens of nearly every size, depending on the choice of rootstock. In colder climates, Siberian crabapple stock is often used, but other rootstocks have been developed in the UK to be trialled in California, proving equally accommodating in both Californian and English climates, so the apple tree may be one of the most resilient of all fruit trees.

Plums, *Prunus domestica*, must also be amongst the most defiantly resilient fruiting trees of all, often the only trees remaining in abandoned gardens. Among dozens of varieties the gages, *P. domestica* subsp. *italica*, stand out for their longevity and tenacity. Pears, *Pyrus communis*, are particularly useful fruit trees, accommo-dating in a wide climate range and, although large trees, they can conform for a small garden, looking smart and performing well espaliered into a cordon or other elegant forms against a wall. I have planted *Pyrus communis* 'Conference' wherever I've gardened with equal success, its pendulous khaki-brown fruits ripening in late autumn. The quince, *Cydonia oblonga*, can either make a handsome tree where there is space or can be espaliered to elevate a very ordinary fence into a thing of beauty that will be festooned with spring flowers, then golden fruits in autumn. The quince hails from the harsh Caucasus and is terrifyingly tough. I grew them in a car park in New South Wales, watered only when someone remembered, and in England

Above: Pyrus communis.

Opposite, clockwise from top left: Prunus cerasus; Ficus 'Brown Turkey'; Cydonis oblonga; Prunus domestica 'Victoria'.

my oldest plants have survived nearly swamp-like conditions by the garden's lake. There are varieties for most climates, including 'Leskovac' and 'Serbian Gold', which I have planted at West Green.

Both the Fig, *Ficus carica*, and the mulberry, *Morus nigra*, are romantically linked to hot lands, but their range extends much further. At West Green House, a tall mulberry produces buckets of deepest red, raspberry-like fruit in the walled garden, and many varieties of figs do well in temperate climates. Give them a warm and sheltered spot and I have noticed they will produce fruit as far north as gardens situated in central England. The reliable F. 'Brown Turkey' performs well and the large fruiting Bavarian fig 'Violetta' is tolerant to - 4°C (25°F). Buy from a nursery to ensure your plant is a female tree, which produces fruit, and then when planted, don't give it the run of a well-mulched flower bed but choose somewhere that it can be confined – in a restricted spot against a warm wall is ideal. In warmer climates the roots of a fig will have to search for water and will keep themselves under control, but in wetter climates the roots must be restricted.

Cherries, *Prunus cerasus* and *P. avium*, grow through a wide range of climates, with sweet and sour varieties fruiting from Scandinavia to Spain, through most of the USA and in New South Wales, Australia. Here cherries were our red berries for Christmas, sour 'Montmorency' or sharp, richly red 'Morello' our shiny red substitutes for out-of-season holly. A mature cherry is a tree of great beauty, but you have to battle with the birds to enjoy its fruit. To win, many gardeners cover their cherry trees with nets, but this does rather detract from the visual appeal.

A mature cherry is a tree of great beauty, but you have to battle with the birds to enjoy its fruit

Vegetables for all gardens

There are very few vegetables that are truly resilient. Many will grow in a range of climates, but they all need nurture. However, a garden without a vegetable patch is somehow rather incomplete, so I've included those vegetables which can flourish, be it with devotion, in gardens climatic zones apart.

A conventional vegetable plot can be extremely water-hungry, so I prefer the style of the traditional European potager where fruit, vegetables, herbs and annuals are grown together for protection and ease of cultivation. Most annual vegetables can be encouraged to grow in most conditions, given appropriate sun and shelter, but to conserve resources it makes sense to grow those that are best for the local climate. Mediterranean vegetables will grow in the far north with protection and a considerable amount of effort, and in the hottest zones with regular water, but it is far better to choose less demanding subjects.

It is common sense to plant vegetables with other plants that make good friends, both thriving in similar conditions. In hot climates, vegetables often need some shelter, growing under the dappled shade of climatically attuned fruit trees, thriving in rich moist soil but adapting to harsher situations. In cooler climates, maximum sun is needed for fruit and vegetables, so fruit trees can be trained to arches, along walls or in free-standing shapes to avoid shading beds.

Among the most tolerant of vegetables, and for its theatrical appearance, I would always include the perennial globe artichoke, *Cynara scolymus*, in a vegetable garden. Although it is usually regarded as a sun-lover, it has thrived in the old walled garden at West Green House where it is used as a decorative and protective hedge with its silver-grey, dissected leaves growing to 1.8m and spiky choke heads in green to purple. Artichokes make decorative pot plants as unpicked chokes turn into jacaranda-blue thistles, but once they

have fruited they should be cut back – in hot climates there are two crops in a year. The unrelated but tolerant Jerusalem artichoke, *Helianthus tuberosus*, is another easy candidate, especially for cool and shady gardens, but it is hard to eradicate once established.

Rhubarb, *Rheum x hybridum*, is dramatic and architectural wherever it is planted, its giant leaves falling gracefully from rosy stalks. The crowns of my plants at West Green have been *in situ* at least 30 years, exposed to all weather, so they must be classified as super-resilient for northern gardens, and my family's garden in southern New South Wales housed some unloved specimens on its dry perimeter.

Pumpkins, *Cucurbita maxima*, can be quite indecently enormous especially the huge orange C. *maxima* 'Quintale', but many are more manageable, such as the

Below: The rampant companions – zucchinis and nasturtiums – provide late summer and early autumn colour.

It is common sense to plant vegetables with other plants that make good companions...

butternut 'Rugosa'. All revel in autumn warmth and I like to use them not only as generous ground cover but also to scramble up and hang down from arches – the grapefruit-sized orange-fruited 'Festival' is a good climber. I like edible squash mixed with the fantastic shapes of ornamental gourds that will lift any vegetable garden from purely functional to wonderfully decorative. All styles of beans and pulses grow perfectly just about anywhere with water, but lettuces and many juicy green salad crops will only behave correctly in cooler climate zones – where the temperature is continually hot many will bolt almost overnight, so there is a need to keep sowing them; it's better to choose selected forms of wild greens in hot gardens.

Many of my favourite seeds originate from growers in Italy, available from popular catalogues, and give excellent results. They offer wild rocket, spinach varieties with coloured stalks and leaves, and endives in many colours and shapes. Zucchini (courgette) flowers that are so scrumptious fried in batter come from *Cucurbita* 'Nano' and 'Verde di Milano' – these long green zucchini produce unending vegetables until the first frost cuts them back.

Many annual flowers also make happy subjects for a vegetable garden, although many will thrive in a less hospitable spot than an enriched vegetable bed. Californian poppy (*Eschscholzia californica*), hollyhock (*Alcea rosea*), nasturtium (*Tropaeolum majus*), pot marigolds (*Calendula officinalis*), cosmos and the everlasting daisy all need scant water. Snapdragons (*Antirrhinum majus*) and sunflowers (*Helianthus annus*), on the other hand, prefer good soil and watering. Planted among the vegetables and nearby fruit trees, they not only look convivial, but together they give a kaleidoscope of colour on economised water, especially alongside one of the toughest vegetables, chard, especially *Beta vulgaris* 'Northern Lights' with ruched, deep green leaves lit by strident stems of yellow, pink, red and orange.

Top left: Eschscholzia californica, a Californian native, is an accommodating plant needing scant water.

Top right Snapdragons in the vegetable garden at West Green House would look equally at home in a Mediterranean garden, as long as they received a little water.

Above: Dahlias and nasturtiums in the Jardin du Plume, Normandy.

Righut: Miscanthus grasses capture both light and movement, giving them a vitality that is irresisitible.

grass gardens

Grasses are amongst the most resilient of all plants. A friend of mine observed that grasses had overtaken garden design like a tidal wave, yet though it seems like a tsunami, their encroachment has been more like global warming, a gradual impact. More than a decade ago, I spent a day beside Chesapeake Bay in Maryland, USA, where the American landscape architect James van Sweden had created urban gardens that, from a distance, became natural extensions of the swathes of native rushes beside the water. On closer inspection, these plantings were as controlled as any European parterre, for he was positioning grasses and perennials, many indigenous, in huge monogamous Cubist patterns that to me looked like a Mondrian painting turned into a domestic garden. What was even more remarkable was that these plantings were around holiday houses where plant choices had to survive irregular care in a climate that see-sawed from snowy winters to hot summers.

James van Sweden had created urban gardens that, from a distance, became natural extensions of the swathes of native rushes beside the water

grass gardens

Near Chicago, van Sweden was remaking the landscape by covering the hillsides with just one or two well-defined drifts of a single native grass. These great rhythmic plantings of prairie grasses were awe-inspiring, but they too had to cope with extremes of dry and ice. I marvelled at this then-new concept of gardening, but reflected what an environmental hazard it would be in dry, fire-prone areas of Australia, in a Californian canyon garden or the dry hills in France, Spain and Greece. Undoubtedly, the grass choices would be climatically viable, but massed plantings of long grass close to a dwelling would be summer tinder boxes in these environments. Despite this caveat, many ornamental grasses are just too practical to dismiss. Not only do they give a sense of life and movement to a garden, but there also is a sense of freedom about them that can loosen the stays of a traditional border design.

In a hot climate, we crave the cool oasis of a green garden, escaping from the brown paddocks or dusty streets to sit under the deep shade of trees, to admire a brilliant burst of flower colour and feel refreshed by pools. But these traditional green oasis gardens are impractical, both environmentally and financially, and require copious water, so fresh gardening and planting styles must evolve to meet a changing climate's insufficiencies. It is a challenge to fit the fashionable russet and brown grasses into this desire for a new style of green garden, and at first I thought it unsolvable, but answers are evolving. By mixing the best-coloured and most environmentally friendly grasses with perennials, the grasses' bulk automatically covers the earth, leaving the perennials' strong colour to make these plantings fresh and inviting.

Many plants that grow happily in dry climates will adapt to the amount of water they can expect and, in a hot climate, a well-prepared bed of organic mulch mixed with a draining gravel will give much of the moisture retention and drainage they need. Conversely, many grasses that grow well in temperate climates will adapt to hotter climes. I recently visited Mary Payne's garden, Lady Farm, which is in a part of England that receives more than sufficient rain. On a gentle slope, amongst the barren rubble of a collapsed tennis court, she was growing a succession of hardy perennials that I knew would survive with minimum water. Each flower I saw that day was native to a very hard habitat, but in a well-drained home in a lusher environment they happily survive excess water and need only minimal care. All of us from sun-drenched lands know the reliability of South African *Kniphofia uvaria*, the tall orange rods of red hot pokers. Here at Lady Farm, their colour was dominant on a late autumn afternoon alongside the spectral *Eryngium bourgatti* 'Picos Blue', its filigree-silver bracts around the amethyst cone-like fingers clutching the last blue balls of echinops. These stood out from the golds and browns of *Coreopsis* daisies and *Verbascum olympicum*, whose spires could have inspired Gaudi's cathedral in Barcelona. This had self-seeded across the slope, often corralled by mounds of the matching grey herbs santolina and artemisia. There was also a variegated form of *Artemisia alba* 'Canescens', its markings irregular green and yellow, often with the miniature golden *Hemerocallis* 'Stella de Oro' as its neighbour.

Above: The intense blue grass *Fesctuca glauca* with the stiff stems of *Verbena bonariensis* set the colour tone in this border of grasses and perennials.

Bottom left: End-of-season eryngiums interrupt bold clumps of miscanthus in the Lady Farm garden.

Bottom right: *Stipa tenuissima* self-seeds its long blond tresses in the grass garden that now covers Lady Farm's old tennis court.

grass gardens

There was nothing particularly new about this random perennial collection – they were all floriferous stalwarts chosen for their sustained flowering season – but what lifted this planting to an inspirational level were the rolling swathes of *Stipa tenuissima* encircling them. This thigh-high graceful grass could be mistaken for over-bleached hair – stroke it and fine strands come away. Voluptuous and cool, it flowed and framed the perennials, masking their inevitable die-back while its own flowing tresses gave movement to the planting, something that could never be achieved by a group of flowering perennials alone. Although it's not a long-lived perennial, this grass self-seeds and is easily pulled and discarded or transplanted as required. *S. tenuissima* has superb manners: commencing its season jade green, it eventually becomes a bleached blonde, holding its form into winter, when it is cut back. It was the marriage between perennials and grass that was inspiring, definitely an equal match, for the splatter of eye-catching blooms seemed like coloured boats on the light spume of the grass sea, a cool and bright planting that would be welcoming on a hot day.

Many of us remember our grandmothers struggling to control huge clumps of pampas grass, *Cortaderia selloana*, mattocks in hand, vowing never to repeat this type of large grass planting, but grasses this huge are now returning. On a pathway to a summerhouse, massive coloured grasses appeared at Lady Farm, giving a very 21st-century twist to a formal planting style. These vast grasses were not looking back to those days of pampas grass but were declarations in a brave new garden, woven confidently throughout the planting. Autumn was high season at Lady Farm, with knee-high mounds of coral-pink *Sedum* 'Autumn Joy' and the pale pink flowers and deep coloured leaves of S. 'Matrona', which was low-growing, but encroaching over the path. Blinding stands of pink echinacea were subdued by a pale mauve mist of lilac perovskia and *Aster* x frikartii 'Mönch', reinforcing the lavender shades. The colour was seductive, but the eye strayed to the skyline

where the drooping, rosy-flowered grass *Miscanthus sinensis* 'Flamingo' was turning silvered pink, and Joe Pye weed, *Eupatorium maculatum* 'Atropurpureum' joined it, its dark purple flowers on reddish stems making an early sunset. Repeated with variations, the planting at Lady Farm weaves tall lyrical grasses and resilient flowers – the whole garden is a *tour de force* in bold form and colour that would willingly accept a drier climate.

Opposite: Tenacious and brilliant early-autumn perennials border the path in this imaginative garden.

Below: A wonderful intermixing of elegant colour is supplied by the hardy *Stipa tenuissima*, artemesia and limonium planted in Lady Farm garden.

grass gardens

Although Mary Payne's climate was mild, the drainage prevented her plants from becoming too wild, keeping them resistant to devastation by wind or spells of heat. When plants from temperate climates are grown with too much moisture in warm, dry climates they can become too lush, too tall, and are liable to shrivel or break in strong heat and hot winds. Whereas you might like to spoil them in cool climates, you'll need to treat them more harshly in the warmth. I recently saw an immaculate recreation of a traditional English, late-summer, herbaceous border in southern France, using all the in-vogue, late-season plants, but grown with minimal water. The fine spikes of *Persicaria amplexicaulis*, *Astrantia major* 'Claret', a magenta geranium amongst many dahlias, *Gaura lindheimeri* and chrysanthemums flourished in the warm, dry climate, but didn't get so large that they were vulnerable.

Grasses can bring a sense of ice-white frost to a hot garden on a late summer's day. In a garden two hours west of Sydney, a circle of *Miscanthus sinensis* 'Graziella', with silver plumes around 1m tall above arching narrow leaves, surrounded a group of *Lagerstroemia indica*, the white form of a small tree that is a froth of little white flowers by midsummer. Together they created a white island in a circular drive. Lagerstroemia are treasured in dry gardens (however, they are not for cooler climes), but it was an artemisia hedge that kept this island bed tidily boxed in. Artemisia plants look horrible when neglected, but are successful and elegant with the slightest attention. *A.* 'Powis Castle', with a froth of petite, silvery grey leaves growing to 60cm, is a vibrant plant for cool gardens – it is reliably hardy as long as it is not subjected to prolonged cold, northern winds and excessive wet.

Above and right: The grasses at Jardin du Plume grow so tall and spectacular one felt like the proverbial dormouse, scurrying through waves of colour, echoed in the undulating forms of the enclosing hedges.

The *Miscanthus* family offers a range of elegant, foamy white grasses …

The similarly proportioned A. absinthium 'Lambrook Silver' is recommended as amongst the hardiest and longest-lived for dry climates, and highly regarded by gardeners in cooler areas, too.

The Miscanthus family offers a range of elegant, foamy white grasses from dwarf varieties to giants 3m tall. I have used drifts of the fountain-like evergreen maidengrass, M. transmorrisonensis, to echo the fall of white water into a pond. Either side of this waterfall stones are piled in an uncompromising formation but this grass' volume, evergreen leaves and curving white tresses, will make this manmade feature more sympathetic to the grassed hills behind. It is an undemanding grass that will cover the site completely and survive on intermittent rainfall. It also grows along and above a wall in this New South Wales' garden's drive, its cascade a contrast to the rigidity of the avenue of *Magnolia grandiflora* rising above it.

In Normandy, France Sylvie and Patrick Quibel have created an extraordinary new garden, Le Jardin Plume. They have taken an exposed field and behind newly planted windbreak hedges have designed a garden in geometric parterres, the majority filled mainly with

grasses capturing every zephyr. Although Normandy is moist, what intrigued me was seeing the grasses and perennials I'd known in gardens in South Africa and New Zealand where they were equally at home, defending themselves in field soils of baked clay

open to howling winds. In Normandy, they were displayed in different compartments of the garden with moods ranging from frivolous to controlled, in field-like areas and modern takes on structured French baroque parterres.

The philosophy of this garden is remarkable. Patrick Quibel describes it as a garden of waves where undulating plants capture the atmosphere's pale light and colour. He likens the grasses to waves and the flowers to salty froth. After looking at the garden for a while, I realised what he meant as the usual solid structure of woody plants was entirely absent. The only linear design was formed by paths either of cut grass, by the hedges or by soil around the square parterres, the height provided solely by the intermassing of grasses and perennials – the one exception was an aged apple tree that had became the garden's central ornament, laden with fruit mirrored in an oblong reflecting pool. The old tree has been used as the concept for another element that will solidify this design in the future. Sixteen sapling apple trees have been planted, one in the centre of each grass parterre, but they were still so young and fine when I visited they seemed to disappear into the atmosphere, so all I saw were the tightly packed, willowy grasses and perennials. Two traditionally designed enclosed parterres, on this early autumn day, were so amassed in grasses and flowers that they gave this planting a total unity. The same plants were repeated again and again, making an effective and co-ordinated design.

Left and below: Sharp, smart mown grass and clipped hedges emphasise the softness of the grasses at Jardin du Plume. In this autumn garden, the grass-shaped leaves of phormiums add solidity to finer grasses whilst the dahlias and nasturtiums supply paintbox colour.

grass gardens

I wandered along paths between parterres like the proverbial dormouse, beneath 120cm-tall asters – the fine *Aster* 'Vasterival', its stems black with mauve flowers, nearly annihilated a stray pinnacle of *Cimicifuga racemosa* var. *cordifolia* 'Purpurea', its 150cm black stems topped with elongated white bottlebrush flowers, all entrapped in fine grasses. Cimicifuga has proved difficult for me, and in my dry garden I'd replace it with the lower-growing 40cm-tall stems of *Sanguisorba* 'Tanna' with its burgundy cones, or perhaps the taller airy plant solidaster, over 70cm tall with narrow green leaves, clouded with cushions of yellow flowers. This plant will flower happily twice a season on minimal water and provide the same impact.

Box, *Buxus*, is the most extraordinary plant. It is the backbone of so many gardens in a wide climate range and at Le Jardin Plume it was not only cut into rhythmic waves rolling between grasses, but also used in the classic way to define parterres, cut into hedges nearly 125cm tall, containing heleniums that were luminous from summer to the first frosts. The marmalade-orange *Helenium* 'Zimbelstern' grew to 120cm tall, supporting dark-stemmed *Dahlia* 'Bishop of Llandaff' and orange-flowering D. 'David Howard'; rich red D. 'Pom of Poms' and single, soft yellow D. 'Pale Yellow' were multiplied many times. The ubiquitous kniphofias appeared, strong and solid *Kniphofia uvaria* 'Nobilis', red K. 'Alcazar' and deep coral K. 'Nancy's Red' – plant these *en masse* and rejoice in the colour. Another tough South African, crocosmia, is an essential enduring summer bulb; here the warm yellow *Crocosmia* x *crocosmiiflora* 'George Davison' and bronze and orange *C*. x *crocosmiiflora* 'Dusky Maiden' were planted alongside *C*. 'Lucifer', a leggy redhead. Acid-yellow euphorbia flowers were cut through by Japanese blood grass, *Imperata cylindrica* 'Red Baron', a fluorescent vermilion leaf with emerald-green slashes. I tried to grow this striking grass at West Green House, over-wintering it in the greenhouse – it did just survive, but it is a warmer-climate garden grass,

at its most flamboyant when the sun's high in the sky.

Central to the jewel-coloured garden was *Miscanthus* 'Pünktchen', an exceptional grass with reddish-pink flower stems. It appeared in each parterre, tall and cloudy amongst many bold, bright and complementary colours. Annuals also rioted through the garden, the last flowers of an orange cosmos were being pushed out of the way by enormous trails of rampant giant nasturtiums in colours from clotted cream to burnt red backed by marbled foliage (probably *Tropaeolum majus* 'Jewel of Africa', that will scramble to 240cm tall). The nasturtium trails spilled over the neat box to bring rampant jungle to the neatly designed beds. Each section of this impressive garden offered a new page of emotions with so many moods and colours – fanciful, vivid, monotone and graceful – but the final section just said steel and elegance: a narrow path led between walls of tightly packed, vertical plumed grasses standing as sturdy as any manmade construction. *Miscanthus sinensis* 'Silver Feather' faced M. 'Grosse Fontaine', and across this grass-walled pool, as dense vertical lines echoed the surrounding grey weatherboard, was decking – simple and potent, creating a totally private space. Le Jardin Plume explores the virtuosity of grasses, opening our minds to their many possibilities.

Above and right: Grasses and the simple faces of Japanese anenomes are the most ephemeral of plantings (right). It is desirable, when designing, to anchor soft plantings with solid structure. Clipped cubes of yew satisfy this need (above) whilst beautiful cobble stones and a charming well-head frame the picture (right) in these English gardens.

grass gardens

Bulbs with grasses

Many of us from warm and dry countries marvel at the beauty of fritillaries in romantic fields, glimpsed beyond garden gates in north European gardens and bold hybrid tulips in formal plantings, as they largely live only on the pages of coffee-table books because there is rarely enough winter cold to allow them to flower. However, many tulip species are native to central Asia and north Africa, so they do not just grow in temperate lands, but will give virtuoso displays in tougher, hotter areas, grown among the shelter provided by grasses. These include the earliest-flowering tulips, the *Tulipa greigii* group originating from Turkestan, with favourites among them the yellow and red T. 'Cape Cod', the orange multi-flowered T. 'Toronto' and the striped-foliaged T. 'Red Riding Hood'. The later-flowering Fosteriana group also reconvenes each year, including the large, creamy white T. 'Purissima' and the petite fire-engine-red T. 'Princeps'.

Species tulips never need to be lifted, nor do *Gladiolus communis* subsp. *byzantinus*, which can colonise and give drifts of magenta flowers among the grass into early summer. These fine, slender-stemmed bulbs are a long way from the flamboyant 'glad' of Barry Humphries' Dame Edna and, crowded with early grasses, bring grace and movement into an informal planting. Other particularly beautiful hardy gladioli are the pure white *Gladiolus* x *colvillii* 'The Bride', the deep red G. 'Robinetta' (*recurvus* hybrid), with its tubular flowers, and the strikingly marked G. 'Charm', with its white throat surrounded by crimson flowers.

Architectural grasses

Grasses planted in strong architectural shapes, juxtaposed like solid inorganic masses, are sheer drama. For me, the colour and shapes of autumn

Below: *Tulipa* 'Red Riding Hood'.

Opposite clockwise, from left: *Tulipa purissima* syn. 'White Emperor'; *Gladiolus* x *colvillii* 'The Bride'; *Tulipa* 'Cape Cod'

… many tulip species are native to central Asia and north Africa, so they do not just grow in temperate lands

Grasses planted in strong architectural shapes,
juxtaposed like solid inorganic masses, are sheer drama

Left: John Coke has planted mixed grasses in a severe formal grid at Bury Farm in Hampshire.

Right: Blue aster and coral red persicaria are vibrant on an autumn afternoon at Lady Farm.

Overleaf: Bold ribbons of Molinia caerulea 'Poul Petersen' at Scampston Hall illustrate perfecty how dramatic bronze grasses look outlined in green.

grasses enhance and magnify the appeal of autumn perennials, giving them bulk and making the autumn garden more voluptuous. Although many of the late summer and autumn grasses are of Junoesque proportions and could swamp a small garden, some, though tall, are still delicate and move diaphanously. A small clump of the golden seedheads of *Stipa gigantea* rising 2m above the spikes of misty lavender perovskia will give the perennial substance without overpowering the garden as the grass's tall flower is light and refined. *S. gigantea* seems climatically impervious, its oat-like wands as thrilling in a garden that receives only 50cm of rain as it is in a north European garden.

At John Coke's garden near Bentley, in Hampshire, a large parterre covers the entire entry courtyard to the house and makes a monumental statement. It is designed to be of substantial-sized rectangular beds, bordered in rusty steel surrounded by thick pebble paths, and a portion of the parterre is planted in just one choice of grass, forming a dense square of eye-high *Calamagrostis* x *acutiflora* 'Karl Foerster' growing in precision as solid building blocks. This is a grass that withstands high temperatures, but here in this cool temperate landscape the planting is surrounded with changing hard materials – an entry path of rectangular paving blocks with the beds encompassed by different-textured stones. The parterres continue with row upon row of rectangles dominated by large mixed grasses. With just gravel, grass and steel, the garden is as bold and dynamic in summer as when coated in frost on a winter's day – a garden suited to every season and a range of climates. The geometric design gives

an impression of a field of grass; it is illusionist and practical, making the grasses easy to maintain whilst giving the sense of infinity. For those who wish to enjoy the sweep and grandeur of grasses, but who must consider the combustible nature of them in areas prone to bush fire, this design could be immensely practical. In a dry climate, bush fires are always a threat, and to plant vast swathes of dry grass in a garden close to the house could be problematic. This garden gives the illusion of far more grasses than there are, an interesting solution for containing their use.

Into this linear design, a silent rectangular pond reflecting light was a calm architectural element amongst this moving mass. A skeletal gazebo merged into the atmosphere, melting into the timelessness of this superb garden. But, as a gardener with roots in a dry climate, what was dramatic were the bronze grasses surrounded by lush mown grass, with the immediate skyline obscured by dense stands of green oaks and other native trees – all cool, refreshing colours against the striking contrast of the deep,

grass gardens

rippling grasses. This is a dream world for dry gardeners, as borders of mown green grass cannot be planned if the rains are late, but we do have a palette of green trees – holm oaks, pepper trees, carob trees – that can supply part of the story. There are also verdant groundcovers stalwartly valiant under burning sun, such as scalloped-leafed horehound, *Marrubium supinum*, a dense carpet of soft grey leaves, or *Teucrium scorodonia* 'Crispum Marginatum', a 35cm dwarf wood sage which could provide grey-green texture against the long grasses.

The beauty and form of grasses is unsurpassed when they fall across hard landscaping to soften the edges, especially over manmade pools, walls and paths. When choosing a grass, consider not only the colour of the surrounding landscape, but also the ease of maintenance and particularly the size of the garden – some of the lyrical catalogue descriptions of grasses can mask their girth. Grasses are easy-maintenance compared with annuals and perennials, but clumps need to be controlled and cut back at season's end, or subdivided for excessive bulk. Some grasses send out runners and others self-seed wilfully and there is always the stray length of grass, fallen from a barrow, like the proverbial hair in the soup lying just where it shouldn't. Grasses in pots add softness to the rigidity of the container and larger grasses film any stark wall or skyline beyond. As roof-garden plants they are not only aesthetically pleasing, but the dry-climate grasses need only minimal watering. No other plant draws us more into the environment, connecting us to the elements, than grass. In the confines of enclosed city living, it is nature's liberator and an invigorating reminder of the natural world beyond.

seaside gardens

With water, a near-subtropical assemblage of species can prosper

The seaside is pure movement – the cresting of waves, the rhythm of grass, sand-sculptured dunes and trees shaped by the winds. Untouched, it is a fragile ecology to be respected, a native vegetation accustomed to its climate, plants bending and flattening into low, cushioned balls or stocky shapes as they adapt themselves to the onshore winds. For many of us they are not landscapes to change or tame, but areas to preserve and lightly augment. Not only are they exhilarating spaces, they are also challenging areas where the surest hand needs to plant to accommodate prevailing salty winds, storms and hot summers, with soils that are frequently just sand and pebble, usually seriously alkaline, and water that is often brackish and limited.

For those fortunate enough to be beginning a new garden in a coastal zone, before calling in the contractors, look closely at the local vegetation within a few miles of the sea. In this environment tempered by coastal breezes and the passing seaside shower, a wider range of plants will flourish. Because these are maritime climates, the frosts so often experienced inland are diminished and, with water, sometimes a near-subtropical assemblage of species can prosper.

Right: Pines overhanging a molten sea create the idealised image of the Mediterranean coast.

Left: Although Tasmania is the last stop before the South Pole, the maritime climate of its coastline allows for the most unexpected plantings. Giant kniphofias, yellow buttons of a rampant santolina, purple spots of lynchis and aloes that look like underwater fish make a surprising combination.

Top: *Romneya coulteri* overtaking sea holly.

Bottom: South Africa's blue agapanthus echo the glimpses of the Mediterranean sea beyond the regional stone pines.

To travellers driving along much of the north Mediterranean shore, the dominant mushroom-like stone pines, *Pinus pinea*, are individual shapes symbolic of the region. Beneath, there is the native grey garrigue, a landscape where the tough golden broom, *Genista garrigues*, grows alongside cistus, rosemary and euphorbias, which have joined flag iris, handsome yuccas and other escaped garden plants, all super-impervious species that can create guidelines for successful regional plantings.

At the other end of the world, under the canopy of the all-pervading eucalyptus forest, a unique native vegetation colonises the Australian coastline. Here are coastal varieties of wattle, our mimosa, a multitude of acacia species in golden shades, grevilleas in many sizes and colours, but all with blooms resembling toothbrushes. There are also masses of callistemons, their flowers rightly called bottlebrushes, and banksia, whose strange ugly flower pods were known to generations of Australian children as 'the big bad banksia men'. People decry the monotony of the coastal Australian bush – and at a casual glance it may seem like that – the species may be almost the same, but most often the variety growing by the coast in warm, central New South Wales will be quite different from those hugging the shoreline in Tasmania as native species have adapted to their precise environments.

On a blustery day in southern England, having walked to the end of a cove with a sharp breeze blowing from the English Channel, I turned to retrace my steps and, instead of looking out to sea, trying to see the coast of France, I began to study the gardens of the old houses that lined the curving road. Most had stone walls as windbreaks and plantings that at times continued the windbreak, lowish green walls of foliage cut to form hedges. The evergreen *Euonymus japonicus* predominated and, where there was more shelter, glossy leaves of *Coprosma repens* were rising to a respectable height. In these sheltered traditional garden borders I noticed some of the hardiest plant survivors, all common in UK gardens. Salt-accepting *Artemisia* 'Powis Castle' brushed drifts of centranthus and the thistle-like *Eryngium agavifolium*, a tough sea holly, sprang up beside cytisus – a golden broom for spring – and silver-leafed helichrysum, a grey herb with a powerful curry smell. Nearby in an area prone to high winds the vegetation was limited to wind-tossed grasses or stunted ground covers, which never grow above the rocks.

Although much of the coastal vegetation I had seen was regionally specific, once acclimatised to similar conditions these plants will cover areas in other climate matches, giving us a large plant vocabulary to choose from. Of course, the use of local grasses, shrubs and trees provides any planting with a sense of place, but modern developers seem to be fixated with the idea of 'ease of living' by the sea, where even the thought of a plant is anathema. Too often concrete paving surrounds the holiday let in its seaside urban plot, with perhaps a small sad collection of unwanted and windswept vegetation.

This is often what we begin with, so by the time we acquire a beachside garden the native planting has been long decimated. Coastal suburbia is often just overrun with lawns of the inevitable kikuyu, *Pennisetum chandestinum* – a green summer grass that adores a warmer coastal climate, and will grow until it overtakes beds, shrubs and the beach, with runners unapologetically climbing up trees. This approach is really unfortunate because a seaside cottage garden can be as low-maintenance as any other; it can be both exciting and the epitome of laid-back living.

For all of us, I'm sure, the early-morning walk along the foreshore brings home assorted treasures of driftwood, stones and shells. In my beachside garden at Dangar Island my collection of washed pebbles gradually filled in the gaps between the weathered, silver-grey railway sleepers, which made the steps

The use of local grasses, shrubs and trees gives any planting a sense of place

Below: A seaside garden in Cornwall.

Opposite, clockwise from top left: Euonymus japonicus 'Microphylla Variegata'; *Artemisia* 'Powis Castle'; *Helichrysum*; *Coprosma repens* 'Picturata'.

seaside
gardens

from the beach, the pebbles creating stripes of different colours and textures. I scattered shells beside the path to become perfect, visual, seaside mulch, suppressing weeds and conserving moisture – a thick, beautiful surface that deserves to be seen. Shells also provide drainage, so plants like small groups of *Dierama*, the angel's fishing rod – perhaps the wine-purple D. 'Raven' or D. 'Eleni', a pale pink flower rising from grass-like leaves – can work well. The lightness of this plant echoes the shells' romantic texture. They crave dry roots and warmth; in cooler climates they can do well planted in the driest spots, in dry gravel or even

between flagstones on a raised position beside a pond. With its pale blue bloom, marked with blue kohl-outlined eyes, *Iris unguicularis* is a tenacious North African iris and one of the first to flower in late winter, hiding amidst grass-like foliage. I pull out those leaves closest to the flower to make it more prominent. This could be a compatible choice above the shells, for it too can withstand the seaside elements. As well as the older, pale-blue-flowering variety there are new varieties in white and purple shades. All need to be cut back and subdivided regularly because the leaves become scraggy.

Below and opposite, from left to right:
Dierama; Iris unguicularis; Eucalyptus
gunnii; Pennisetm villosum.

Washed rounded pebbles in all sizes not only echo a beach theme but will also create a moisture-preserving background for grouped grasses. Try the gentle arching stems of *Pennisetum villosum* 'Cream Falls'; its ears or tails of white down are impossible not to touch. Or bring the sea closer with groups of *Leymus arenarius* 'Blue Grass'. Both grasses can withstand winds, rain and dry spells, they form mannerly mounds no taller than around 50cm and look superb in repeat plantings. A well-known English seaside garden was created by British film director and actor Derek Jarman beside a pebbled seashore on the south coast. He spaced a

personal collection of plants and artefacts through a continuous pebbled area. This garden was entrancing for me because the unceasing harmony of the stones kept a visual beat going once the immediate interest of the flowers and collected jetsam had faded.

I have always admired *Romneya coulteri*, the largest white poppy, its petals the texture of Japanese silk fluted flat around a raised yellow eye, on 2m grey stems with silver-grey leaves. In mild seaside gardens it thrives, some say too well, but a good group catching the wind is to be remembered. I'd emphasise its clear white by

seaside gardens

mulching around it with a scattering of white marble chips or the whitest stones to shine as brightly as the sea. A pebbly seaside garden could be an ideal home for the poppy, for it can be very invasive when given ideal conditions.

Where there is heat, coastal showers for humidity, no frost and a regular water supply, plant choice can be frenetic even only minutes behind the sea front. In these conditions an assemblage of plant collections can give illusions of different places, and it is irresistably tempting to create a lush-looking, tropical island garden. The hardy cabbage tree palm, *Cordyline australis*, gives a marvellous jungle feeling. In their native habitat cordylines form wild leaf-heads, making a garden look like something from *South Pacific* with their 1m-tall leaves radiating out from a single branch. Sadly they have been overused by designers as tough 'modern'

plants over the last couple of decades and are now too often relegated to trash, neglected and unloved, so be kind and return them to the wild where they can be magnificent. *Fatsia japonica* is another deep green shrub growing to 4m to give tropical style with its dominant palmate leaves; it is extremely hardy in a maritime position although it would welcome the protection of a group of plants for it can scorch and be troubled by ever-blowing winds. Mature plants flower with a spray of cream umbels – a very elegant autumn addition.

Lily-style flowers provide a thrilling tropical look to seaside gardens. The New Zealand rock lily, *Arthropodium cirratum* 'Parnell' is pure white within large, sage-green leaves. *Gloriosa superba* 'Rothschildiana', a crimson-red-edged yellow spider lily, is exuberantly flamboyant. According to some sources this spider lily is tender, but perhaps I have been lucky for I have had it flower

in the garden in midsummer protected by associated planting. It may be more important to check that it does not become invasive in warmer coastal climates.

Trees are invaluable in coastal gardens to break the wind, provide shade and connect a garden to the landscape. Giant trees can look striking but they tantalise the wind and are a mixed blessing, especially as their branches are prone to snap. Smaller, less rigid trees will break the wind and filter the breeze. Silk trees, *Albizia julibrissin*, have foliage similar to the

Opposite and above, from left to right: Romneya coulteri; Cordyline australis; Arthropodium cirratum 'Parnell'; Gloriosa superba 'Rothschildiana'.

Overleaf: Albizia julibrissin.

Where you have heat, coastal showers for humidity, no frost and a regular water supply, plant choice can be frenetic …

jacaranda and extraordinarily lovely, silky, powder-puff-shaped, pink flowers that are delightful to touch. These trees are quick-growing to a maximum of 8m. They are not long-lived but are captivating in small groups with their spreading branches, and flower best with minimum water in poor soil. This is a tree I'd choose to lead my eye along a path towards the sea view and revel in their spent flower blossoms underfoot for they are totally come-hither plants, demanding a closer look. But where the wind is strong, I'd choose a sturdy hedge, perhaps in blue to harmonise with the sea beyond, specifically the ice-blue foliage of *Cupressus glabra* clipped to a suitable height.

A terrace and a beach house conjure up relaxing images of days spent enjoying the sun, gentle shade and warm breezes, but as they are open to the elements they are subject to temperate extremes and the materials used in any hard landscaping need to be as carefully considered as any planting. Pale-coloured marble on a terrace is luxurious, but at noon when the sun is high overhead it reflects dazzle from the sea beyond, creating a blinding light, and it can be white-hot. Pot plants struggle to survive intense, reflected heat and everyone needs sunglasses just to move across the terrace. Many marbles also stain easily so careful placing of pots is necessary on marble surfaces – and try to avoid fruits that fall, berries that attract birds (for the birds do not have the best table manners) and unfortunately some flowers with strong-coloured petals.

Plate-glass windows frame magnificent seascapes and toughened-glass pool fences allow the enjoyment of the surrounding view, but sea breezes bring salt spray and constant cleaning is needed. Shiny metal handrails will conduct heat as well as cold, so will brushed steel planter pots and polished metal garden furniture. Mirror ornaments are capricious: although they can bring added reflection and increased depth to a garden, they can also be fire conductors and blinding when the sun is high in warmer climate zones. Materials that can make striking architectural statements in the right situation can be unfriendly when used in suntraps of defused heat, both for plants and people. Natural materials – cane, wood and terracotta – neither trap the sun nor retain as much heat and are therefore much more amenable.

Sympathetic walls of water or plants can mitigate searing summer heat. Walls of stone, slate and pebbles filmed with water are now accepted features and, in warmer lands, sempervivems and other friendly creeping and low-growing succulents have covered roofs for years.

Decorative grapevine leaves or the large leaves of the rampantly climbing Chinese gooseberry vine, *Actinidia deliciosa* syn. *Chinensis lispida*, could be grown on free-standing wall frames to break the concentrated heat from a sea-enhanced sun reflected on to shiny surfaces. Green-covered walls are increasingly being used in designs for urban areas to help to regulate the rise in temperature caused by so many heat-absorbing hard materials and I have become intrigued with the idea of using the same techniques in baking seaside gardens. Commercially available 'growing walls' are vertical frameworks where plants are inserted into a regular pattern of planting envelopes filled with a grainy material that is fed and watered by a controlled drip system. Most of the 'growing walls' I know have used plants of cool temperate climates, but I believe this technology may provide interesting answers for walls that conduct heat in the summer and look bleak and windswept in winter by using plants that relish a wider climate range.

When designing in a seaside environment that is controlled by wind and direct sun, think about this climate's effects on the plants. They may tolerate the conditions, but they may grow and develop differently from their relatives planted in less stressful environments. A plant's cycle can be accelerated by sun: it often matures quickly and may have a comparatively short lifespan. Plants may be truncated by constant wind movement — my seafront *Teucrium fruticans* was almost bonsaied; I should have planted *T. azureum*, which is just as appealing, with a deeper blue

flower, and is wind tolerant. Choose from the many plants that have adapted to hold their shape while fronting a prevailing wind — *Grevillea rosmarinifolia*, with its ruby flowers, is impervious on cliffs and ledges and escallonia is another evergreen for a coastal garden, especially the deep rose-flowered *Escallonia* 'C. F. Ball' that flowers throughout midsummer.

When establishing a seaside garden, consider how to conserve moisture in the soil. First enrich the base soil, whether it is sand, gravel or loam, with good organic compost and only then add any decorative mulch to combat the leaching of prevailing winds and seasonal storms. Augment the plants' nutritional requirements with a slow-release fertiliser just before the growing season commences. Weeds, like the plants, will bolt away if nurtured in an accelerated climate, so before laying the decorative mulch it is a good idea to lay membrane on the prepared soil, then place the shells, pebbles or other chosen topping upon it.

When establishing plants it is helpful to protect the initial plantings with protective screens. Low panels of woven wattle or willow placed windward are effective and decorative. Sturdy, stretched horticultural cloth or even an old car tyre or two will break the wind and prevent it from burning and drying the new plants. If the garden is on the ocean front, check that the plants do not object to salinity in the soil and that they can accept a salt-bearing wind that may scorch the flower or leaf. If a plant does not like alkaline soil, it will soon react with yellowing leaves. Mulching a bed can often hide how much wind has dried out a plant, so do check, especially in winter. Never be afraid to try to move a plant to find its right location.

Right: Giant agaves and cordylines contend with salt-laden winds on the Mediterranean coast, and can be resilient in sheltered coves of the English coastline too.

> Choose from the many plants that have adapted to hold their shape while fronting a prevailing wind…

a seaside garden for villa christina

I s life completing its full cycle? Perhaps so, for now, three decades later, I am in the process of planting the most resilient garden. It has to be a tiny patch filled with obliging trouble-free Mediterranean plants, but still a flowering garden for an Indian summer devised for a gardener who just wants to sit in the sun. This time it will be a garden with not a eucalyptus in sight but shaded by stone pines, *Pinus pinea*, perched on a cliff with the fabled Mediterranean Sea at its feet. Although this garden is place-specific, its whole ethos is resilience.

For I too have joined those who yearn for a place in the sun (it took fifteen years to succumb to the UK cold), retreating as time permits from a lush, high-maintenance north European garden to plant once again the flowers that thrive with neglect. This is a miniscule project, just pockets in a terrace, a retaining wall to cover and green, then three shallow shelves to plant. As a holiday garden it will be a challenge to maintain, for not only will it be abandoned for months, but the sun filtered through pine needles will also create dry shade and there will be the ever-prevailing sea winds.

Right: This is my first snap of the terraced view from Villa Christina, surrounded by stone pines, with the blue Mediterranean at my feet.

Although this garden is place-specific, its whole ethos is resilience

Left: Planted in a luxury garden, *Phoenix canariensis* is a wonderful tree for a large area. It would be too big for my little garden.

*Clockwise, from left: I will be hedging
Pittosporum tobira, and encouraging
the wild Asphodelus aestrivus and
Camassia leichtlinii to invade
my terraces.*

During the hot season, the terrace plants in their
shallow soil will combat the sparkling reflection from
the sea below and the heat generated by the paving
tiles all around. Survival can be guaranteed only by the
plant selection – all the delightful plants (even those
attuned to dryness, but needing a weekly water) that
must be sprayed, constantly kept clipped or nurtured
cannot be considered. It has to be a garden of resilient
plants that accept long, hot summers, a coolish, wet
winter period of around four months and constant
salt-laden wind, blowing immediately onto it, for it
is the 'front stalls' with the sea absolutely beneath. To
find the right plant collection I began by prowling the
local nurseries for, although geographically I will be
planting in the Mediterranean climate zone, each area,
whether it has high mountains, coves or prevailing
winds, creates its own microclimate and so inevitably
some plants excel locally over others.

Eye-catching were the nursery plants geared for the
luxury market – the sentinel palm, *Phoenix canariensis*,
mountainous palm groups of *Chamaerops humilis* and
ancient olives in tubs to be lifted only by fork-lift
truck for instant gardens with water and staff laid on.
But I was looking for young plants with sufficient
roots to acclimatise, anchor firmly and grow happily
alone. However, the nursery visits answered many
questions – from the car window I noticed a glossy,
evergreen hedge with fists of small, creamy white
flowers that seemed to be planted everywhere. It was
Pittosporum tobira, a plant that relishes coastal salt winds
as well as inland dry sun and shade, and it has a most
useful dwarf form, *P. tobira* 'Wheelers Dwarf', around
1m tall. Another local native is *Rhamnus ludovici-salvatoris*,
currently a very 'in' dry-climate plant, for it is dense
with small, dark shiraz-coloured leaves that clip well
into edges and mounds, but untended is still a fine
compact shrub. My first visit coincided with spring,
when fields and terraces were invaded by a tall,
shell-pink spike resembling a large branched camassia
that rose from a rosette of grey sword-shaped leaves.

a seaside garden for
villa christina

It was *Asphodelus aestivus*, which is cut back after flowering ends to disappear and then regenerate. Wild garlic, *Tulbaghia violacea*, also prospered and a group of chincher-inchee, *Ornithogalum thyrsoides*, the black-eyed, white-petalled flowers, hanging loosely from their umbrella formation, stood bravely beside the roadside wall.

Looking at nurseries and what thrives in the local countryside provides invaluable information about a range of plants that will grow and be beautiful in abandonment. A path along the clifftop borders my highest garden terrace and I have debated the selection of plants here endlessly. *Bupleurum fruticosum* is a shrub of dull green, but with fine yellow flowers so useful for flower arranging; as a Mediterranean native growing to over 2m it could have been perfect. Then I thought of *Euryops pectinatus* that has survived the most rugged gardens, growing to a 1m high mound of golden daisies, the flowers dense above fine, grey-green leaves. Totally unfussy about soils, fertilisers or pests, it copes well with all but the coolest climates to flower through late autumn into almost summer in a continuous display, until a sharp haircut into the wood when flowering ends.

> When I purchased the Villa Christina, I was overawed by the views and the potential…

When I purchased the Villa Christina, I was overawed by the views and the potential this small project offered. I'd looked at the terraces and registered only that a prostrate rosemary, several *Agave americana* and a handsome yucca were the prominent inhabitants, but on a return visit I looked more closely and found the most 'bonsaied' *Teucrium fruticans* growing, its height I presumed truncated by the wind. So although this climate was similar to that of Dangar Island, the suitability of *T. fruticans* was suspect. Later that afternoon, I thought I saw something moving amongst the pines on the cliffside. It was a reconnoitring party of feral goats, obviously a reconnaissance party to discover what delicacies I would carefully plant for them to chew. All thoughts of soft grey teucrium departed and I decided immediately on an impervious line of white oleander, disastrous for sheep, and goats too I hope! This tough, warm-climate plant, super-resistant to sea winds, will make my boundary hedge here, perhaps not a very original choice for a difficult locality, but very practical.

Left: Agaves in pots look bold and striking and you don't need to worry about them drying out.

Opposite, from left to right: Tulbaghia violacea; Ornithogalum thyrsoides; Bupleurum fruticosum; Euryops pectinatus.

There seems to be a yucca variety to suit the climate of most seaside locations, ranging from a warm country's coastline to sheltered coves in southern England

The two small, elongated terraces cut into the near-vertical rockface have minimal soil. In the highest a *Yucca rostrata* will be planted – a spherical ball of innumerable, long, grey-blue leaves topped by a 60cm bell tower of waxy, white flowers. This is a plant to be multiplied, many times, to form repeat silhouettes against the sea beyond. There seems to be a yucca variety to suit the climate of most seaside locations, ranging from a warm country's coastline to sheltered coves in southern England. There will be a whole patch of blue-grey sword leaves when the blue-leafed *Kniphofia* 'Jenny Bloom' is placed beside the yucca, dramatic with a pale coral poker, making a bed of dominant but inhospitable spires. Pokers in all their colours – green, gold-orange and bi-colours – are invaluable plants, colonising in the poorest soils, and flowering after drought and snow as long as they have good drainage. Truthfully, I never used to rank them too highly, but

since discovering the charmingly coloured 'Jenny Bloom' I've been converted.

I chose these resilient plants because the narrow terrace is scarcely more than a ledge to garden on with a staggeringly precipitous drop below, and as the ledge is just below the path I trust these plants will act as a deterrent for a too-adventurous explorer. Although the ledge will be given a good layer of soil and mulch before the plants arrive, the topography means that planting it is not a job I will want to repeat.

The next tiny ledge will be even more of a challenge, for whatever trailing plant falls from here will be the background for innumerable al fresco occasions, and the wall behind the ledge must be curtained in planting too. Like a silver ghost in the twilight, *Chamaerops humilis* var. *cerifera* forms clumps of graceful fans. I first saw this

Top left: *Verbena rigida* f. *lilacina* 'Lilac Haze'

Opposite: *Chamaerops humilis* var. *cerifera*

tree, sometimes known as the blue Mediterranean fan palm, in a friend's garden above Marbella, in southern Spain. It survives drought, heat, occasional snow, sun, shade and poor soil. I've chosen smallish specimens of this atmospheric plant to be placed high on my ledge, away from passing foot traffic as the palm fronds are sharp. Although in maturity it really will be too large for this space, it will take about two decades to reach its maximum 4m height. This marvellously architectural plant survives in the milder climate of southern England in sheltered areas, its fronds growing to 1m. It looks entirely lush, the epitome of the jungle, but in fact this palm really doesn't like the tropics.

In front of what will now be three rows of silvery plants inhabiting the tiny top terrace, I shall plant a pure white flower as sharp as the light of the sea below. The navy-eyed *Osteospermum fruticosum* is a must here because although it grows in cool northern lands in summer, winter cold kills it, but here, flowering from spring through to winter in the Mediterranean, it will need only an occasional trim, giving a never-ending flower mass all season. The pale lilac flowers of *Verbena rigida* f. *lilacina* will thread through the daisy, accompanying it down the wall, an accommodating plant through a wide climate range. The two make sociable bedmates, both enjoying some mulch, and they prefer being left alone and eventually cut back when the gardener wishes. They will provide a massed flower curtain to obliterate dry stone, softening the walls and creating a refreshing ambience. Alternatively, an erodium, perhaps *Erodium chrysanthum* 'Cotswold Cream' with coin-spot flowers above silvery fern-like leaves, and tolerant of a wider climate range, could be tried. The best thing about that little flower is that it will bloom in late season when I can see it after the garden closes at West Green House.

Now at terrace level, in four square gaps among the tiles, a repeat grouping of five plants will appear, as islands to break the hard texture of tile, but placed

to allow space for chairs in small plant groups that will not impede the view. A 30cm raised edging must surround each plot to hold a mulched soil (for the terrace surface is on rock) to support the group of five plants in each. A teenage olive tree, *Olea europaea*, the biblical symbol of a new life and hope, will make a spindly background and is an obvious choice as it is attuned totally to the environment, making a perfect foil for the low fronds of a cycad, a plant renowned as a living fossil. Easily obtained in Mediterranean nurseries, the two popular choices, *Cycas circinalis* and *Cycas revoluta*, have deep green, graceful fronds that grow slowly in either sun or shade. These plants, somewhere between a palm and a fern in appearance, do need some moisture, so I will apply water crystals and soil additives to the mulch, then ring up a neighbour to check on them when I am not there!

Top left and right: Perhaps one day my seedling olive trees will produce fine fruit like this. However, I know the star jasmine should flower and be beautiful and wax-like by the first season.

I'm sure they'll survive, as there is moisture in sea mists and occasional rain and, already, I have found a surviving plant there on the abandoned terrace, obviously having weathered years of neglect, growing bravely in too small a pot on the terracotta surface. These fine plants are for gardens in the sun, but the pride-of-place specimen for a greenhouse in cooler lands. The slim, evergreen leaves of my favourite *Agapanthus* 'Snowball', just 30cm tall, with heads laden with white flowers, will act as a ground cover at *Cycas revoluta*'s feet. Experience tells me it will be content, for these smaller agapanthus not only cope with drought conditions, but selected varieties also seem to be contending with many climate extremes, including England's snow. Then I'll add another Mediterranean native, the spreading sage-leaf rockrose, *Cistus salviifolius* 'Prostratus', an evergreen massed with tiny, grey leaves hosting small, single, round flowers, white with golden stamens, and spreading 120cm to breaking the hard tile surface.

A large pergola covers the central terrace, filtering the noonday light in summer, casting the shade that a hot climate craves. At first, I thought of creating a dazzling spectacle in shocking colour with two bougainvillea plants, cultivars to be chosen when in flower so as to find the brightest pink and the most intense red that will intertwine to make its hood. The poorer the soil, the higher the temperatures, and the less they are fussed with – all these make for a happy bougainvillea, but sitting in a neighbour's garden I was reminded that strong winds can boisterously toss their numerous papery flowers everywhere, so they are not right for my exposed position. Their brilliant

Wandering through the village,
magnificent tubs of deep green leaves
take pride of place outside doors

colour makes them a number one plant for the needy
sun worshipper, but their thorns and vigorous growth
are negatives, as well as the damage strong winds
wreak on them, so again it was time for reconsid-
eration. What is more legendary for such a situation
than a grapevine? The image of a soporific afternoon,
gazing at one's own bunches of grapes is unbeatable,
but here too the wind could spoil the reverie, so I'm
almost certain the pergola will be cloaked with the
star jasmine, *Trachelospermum jasminoides*. It is compact,
shiny and not at all messy, its leaves are high-gloss
green and its flowers innumerable white stars. I have
grown this elegant, evergreen creeper by the sea north
of Sydney, and in an inland cool temperate garden
where it had to endure dry spells, irregular watering
and some frost. In a cooler climate it would be happier
along a sheltered and warm wall, but I'm sure here it
will acquiesce and be adaptable, for it is always well
behaved, growing in full sun or part shade, with just a
prune after flowering to keep it trim.

It is said that a pool is a mirror of our heavenly
dwelling, and on a thirsty day the sound of water
certainly seems heaven-sent, so a pool is a garden
must, if possible. Space decrees that my pool will be a
trough against one wall, fed by recirculated water from
a polished tap placed close to the water where the tap's
small flow will be quietened – for me the sound of
falling water can be noisy and infuriating in confined
spaces. The water will be collected from winter rain
on the roof and held in a slim-line tank camouflaged
beneath the trough. The pump will be a simple
garden-centre model where clean water is maintained
by continuous movement and a few fistfuls of salt.
A small swimming pool will also be installed on this
level terrace, but separated from the outdoor living
space by the house. Reached from the kitchen door,
this terrace will be firmly enclosed by fences of local
woven reed on two sides, with the smallest greenhouse
– a polite name for shelves protected on three sides by
glass to nurture a few geraniums. The geraniums will

provide a splash of colour to be grown on and enjoyed during the holiday, then handed on to a neighbour when it's time to lock up.

Another simple vivid flower is the pot marigold, a startling orange-gold that relishes the sun. It survives on almost no water and will make a no-nonsense pot plant in this garden. Wandering through the village, I have seen magnificent tubs of deep green leaves taking pride of place outside doors, filled with lush and wide-leafed aspidistras, at home in this climate and obviously practical in the salt-laden air. Cannas too, those tall and vivid flowers which are used in street plantings in many a warm climate, were regal outside other houses. I'm resisting grouping major plant pots near my doors or on the terrace. They can look beautiful but are always a heartache unless you are present to tend them. Even with the best dripper systems, timers fail if the power is interrupted and this

happens occasionally here, the cause usually something as simple as the neighbouring donkey scratching himself on the electricity pole!

At the base of the house I will not resist a small patch of *Iris pallida* with mauve-blue flowers and white-striped leaves, planted with mushroom-like mounds of the incredibly blue grass, *Festuca glauca*, at their feet. This grass is impervious to sea spray and absolutely trouble-free. I like only to cut back its fine silver-brown spent flowerheads in late summer and subdivide the plants after three years or they begin to take on a pot-bound look. Perhaps I'll have a surrounding ground cover of grape hyacinths, *Muscari*, which naturalise easily here.

Bulbs geared for spring, summer or autumn flowering are good choices for neglected gardens, to be tucked in and forgotten if planted in well-drained soil. The bulbs will flower, die back and regenerate in their

Far left: Cordylines, cycads and *Chamaerops humilis* are lush and resilient in this maritime climate.

Left: *Muscari* will naturalise easily at Villa Christina and are also happy in cool temperate climates.

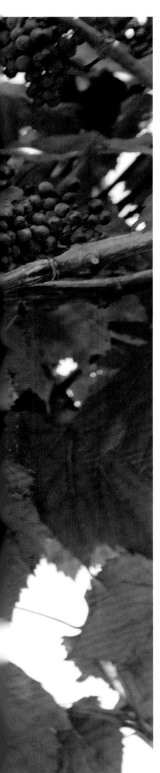

season with no attention from the gardener. I'll try blue *Brodiaea elegans*, 35cm tall with fine stems and bells to flower in midsummer, and for the autumn *Sternbergia lutea*, a yellow flower that rises directly out of the ground and resembles a crocus – both need sun and drought. In spring, another Mediterranean wonder is *Scilla peruviana*, a large cone of deep, dark blue flowers rising from a rosette of shiny, deep green leaves. It truly has the wow factor.

These bulbs will be beneath three fig trees, with espaliered branches on lines of wire to cover some less appealing masonry. I know that figs will flourish because a few metres above my house is the track where the donkey is tethered to the informal electricity pole. This pole has become amalgamated with a venerable fig tree that shades the donkey and what remains of its shed too!

Pomegranates could do well here as they need warmth, survive dry spells and will not mind the shade of the pines. The date palm, olive, pomegranate, fig and the grapevine, all trees of the Bible, are climatically exact for this garden. Perhaps, if I can find a spot for each one, they may help to make my tiny house a true paradise surrounded by the plants of a paradise garden.

Although this garden is tiny and the plant choices limited, I have still tried to create a garden in colours to harmonise with the situation. As the sea dominates its position, I have chosen plants that continue the eye on to the sea's never-ending blue, its white crests and silver sheen. The selected plants are all

Opposite: 'Let us get up early to the vineyards; let us see if the vine flourish, whether the tender grape appear, and the pomegranates bud forth: there will I give thee my loves.'
Song of Solomon 7:12

Below: *Scilla peruviana*.

low-maintenance, so secateurs for pruning and dead heading can just about remain in a bottom drawer and there will be enough plant volume to stifle most weeds. Although all are tough, resilient and should be trouble-free, they are attractive, but in the spaces around the house where I will relax, the plants are all soft-textured leaves and gentle flowers. I am definitely looking for a quiet life.

Bulbs geared for spring, summer or autumn flowering are good choices for neglected gardens …

recommended
resilient plants

This is a very personal collection of extra plants that
have proved resilient for me, intended
just to be a useful starting point.

Arbutus unedo

Irish strawberry tree

Height: to 10m

I'd always thought that the name was a delightful misnomer, for I knew this tree as coming from the Mediterranean, but it is native to the south west of Ireland too with family members in the northwestern USA also.

This is a gold-star resilient evergreen tree, most commonly growing to around 5 or 6m or can be pruned into a multi-stemmed shrub. The tree has an attractive, rounded shape with rounded, glossy, dark green leaves and clusters of pinkish-white flowers that turn into orange-red spherical fruits with rough skins. Show off its handsome, flaking, reddish-brown bark by keeping the lower branches pruned.

Although it will tolerate wind, plant this strawberry tree in a sheltered position, if possible, to ensure a good showing of flowers that are at their best in late autumn although they appear at intervals throughout most of the year. It prefers a lime-rich soil but will tolerate most conditions including rain as well as semi-drought, growing in warm-dry regions as well as areas prone to quite severe frost.

Catalpa bignonioides

Indian bean tree

Height: to 10m

With its huge, lime-green leaves and bunches of foxglove-like flowers, the Indian bean tree seems too exotic to survive extreme temperatures, but with care it's an accommodating tree. Round-headed and architectural, this tree bears large leaves that start pale green and turn to yellowy lime, alongside white, trumpet-shaped flowers in early summer that are followed by long, brown bean pods.

My tree at Kennerton Green was well nurtured in a raised and mulched bed to ensure good drainage. Watered regularly once a week during the hot season, it was in a row of huge, thirsty trees and it thrived amongst the competition. Perhaps not as resilient as some trees in the UK, it is reliably hardy to -15°C(5°F) if given a sheltered position and a sunny spot, and warrants a place for its shape, its brilliant foliage and its flowers.

Cercis siliquastrum

Judas tree

Height: to 8m

Spectacular people, objects or places always attract gossip, and the stunning, magenta, pea-shaped blooms of this tree, appearing on bare stems in the dull days of late winter before the leaves open, are certainly brilliant. Perhaps that is why it became saddled with the legend as the tree from which Judas hanged himself.

A rounded, spreading tree, cercis can also be trained up a pillar or a pergola to show off the stunning blooms sprouting directly from old growth. Heart-shaped leaves and reddish pods develop after flowering in earliest spring in warmer areas, later in cool gardens. It is best to buy the tree in bloom to ensure its colour, which can range from deep red through pink to white.

Cercis will accept dry and warm conditions even into the tropics, but doesn't like to be crowded. In cooler climates it may need protection from cool winds; soil should be well-drained and fertile.

Cercis canadensis, the forest pansy, has beautiful purple leaves and deep crimson or pink flowers.

Chamaecyparis spp.
False cypress
Height: various

Chamaecyparis spp., the false cypress, look as if it has just come from the hairdressers, for the immaculate layers of evergreen foliage make precise cones ranging in height from 40m to 60m, some rising from handsome broad bases, others just narrow columns. The range of cultivars is immense, with the best-known range being *C. lawsoniana*, the Lawson cypress.

Lawson cypresses are available in shades of green, blue and gold, the gold-frosted *C. obtusa* 'Crippsii' is popular. The dwarf forms *C. pisifera* 'Boulevard' are just a 2m high cone designed by nature for a pot.

I personally like the 'Filifera' range whose leaves have been described as 'trailing dreadlocks'. The false cypress trees with their low, shaped and feathery sprays, all densely packed to form a compact shrub or tree, will accept most soils however, if there is added compost they are most appreciative. Most cultivars are resolute, with young trees needing some water during the driest periods, but mature trees have proved resilient during most temperature extremes.

The cypress can be subject to cypress canker that turns the branches brown and eventually kills it; I have faced this problem, with the advice of experts, but never with success. Grubbing out the diseased trees was a large exercise, so today I resort to placing these distinctive trees as individual specimens.

Chimonanthus praecox
Wintersweet
Height: to 4m

The yellow flowers of wintersweet to me do not look very exciting, but the winter fragrance is sublime. Small, open deciduous trees are studded in winter with yellow blossom blooming directly from the old wood. Often these ragged and waxy, deeply scented flowers are the only blooms visible on raw winter days, so the tree is worth growing for that alone. My British trees started life exposed to open fields, buffeted by cold winds and untended in a drained but average soil, and survived to flower beautifully. Ideally you should plant hardy wintersweet in an open sunny spot in well mulched soil. It tolerates heat and minimal watering once established.

Chionanthus spp.

Fringe tree

Height: 5–10m

I have never grown the exquisitely blossomed Chinese fringe tree, *Chionanthus retusus*, but when life became overwhelming when I worked at the Sydney Opera House, I would often walk into the adjoining Botanic Gardens and just gaze at this remarkable small tree in bloom, covered in a feathery mass of white flowers that eclipse the leaves. The flowers of the American fringe tree, *C. virginicus*, are arguably less brightly white but still give the effect of a thorough covering of gossamer. Other chionanthus are tender and evergreen, but both these deciduous species are cold-hardy as far north as the southern counties of the UK, and they are becoming widely used in parts of the US as beautiful street trees as they tolerate urban pollution.

Fringe trees need some water, and like their roots in rich soil with adequate drainage. They prefer slightly acidic soils and some shelter and I think they are best grown in front of a mixed group of trees both for protection and because they are rather unprepossessing when they are in their glorious flowering phase. But if you have the right situation, a fringe tree is a stunning addition to any garden. Leave the tree room to spread into a broad, rounded shape.

Corylus avellana

Hazel

Height: to 5m

The garden of the Priory de Notre Dame de Orson in central France is a recreation of a medieval garden where coppiced hazel canes form its fences, arches, plant supports, edgings and seats. Hazel has been an important tree in country life for centuries, grown for its nuts, for hedging and supports. Some forms have attractive coloured leaves and the yellow catkins are a joy in spring.

Hazel is agreeably hardy, happy in a warm Mediterranean climate or in cooler conditions, coping with any soil as long as it is well-drained. Prune right back in winter, or leave one-year-old wood for fruiting varieties.

C. avellana 'Contorta' has contorted and twisted branches that are a must for a winter garden. *C. maxima* is grown for the best nuts, known as filberts. *C. maxima* 'Purpurea' has deep purple leaves.

Cotoneaster spp.

Height: to 5m

Truly resilient, cotoneasters will survive in almost any conditions, so although they are not my favourite small trees or shrubs they are definitely worth considering, particularly as they have good flowers and berries and are evergreen in warmer conditions, semi-evergreen in cooler areas. There's a huge range; all appear completely hardy, not fussy about water, tolerant of most soil conditions, and happy in sun or part shade.

Cotoneaster frigidus is, I think, the best. It makes a handsome small tree to 5m tall with gently arching branches covered with white flowers in spring and large red berries in autumn.

The shrubby *C. horizontalis* is an excellent form. It seems happy in gravel, sand and clay soils, hot sun and wind and accepts cool, damp weather and frost. Its fan shape looks neat and eyecatching trained against low walls, but it is not reliably evergreen in cold climates. It makes excellent ground cover too, its rigid structure fanning out to cover an area more than 1m wide, with dense berries in autumn and tiny, pink and white spring flowers above small, rounded, green leaves.

Cotinus coggygria
Smokebush
Height: to 5m

Clouds of dusty, taupe, smoke-like flowers billow through the reddish-purple leaves of cotinus in the summer months, a deciduous small tree I have planted in hostile spots in both gardens. In Australia it is on a dry clay bank and in the UK in a very low bed open to the wind where it has survived equally well. It needs reasonable drainage and a well-mulched soil, but will adjust to a sparse water regime. To keep the flowers within sight rather than hidden by abundant foliage, prune severely in winter.

C. coggygria 'Royal Purple' has the deepest purple leaf. C. coggygria 'Young Lady' has large, pink-tinged flowers in summer. C. 'Golden Spirit' has good yellow foliage.

Crataegus spp.
Hawthorns
Height: to 8m

Along England's roadsides in spring the white or deep pink flowering hawthorns are a perfect Maytime image. These compact, rounded deciduous trees have neat, small, dark green, shiny leaves and very thorny stems. They are often grown as hedges and will grow in warmer climates, but some forms are severely prone to pest damage where there is heat.

Hawthorns are hardy, drought-resistant, content in poor soils, and also suitable for cold problem areas. They will grow anywhere except in waterlogged soil.

C. laevigata 'Paul's Scarlet' is a species hawthorn grown widely in the Mediterranean zone. It produces masses of double crimson blooms on a rounded, compact tree with attractive, shiny leaves and a mass of bright red autumn berries that stay on the tree for months. Useful as a specimen plant or incorporated into a hedge.

C. monogyna, common hawthorn or quickthorn, is a good form for warmer climates as it is little troubled by pests. Two of these fine trees grew in the garden at Kennerton Green; their neat, rounded shape cast deep shade when needed in summer and they produced their massed white flowers with pink anthers at the end of spring, a bonus flowering after the other blossoms had finished. They are excellent trees but be careful in their placement as the only way to describe their perfume is public lavatory. Their autumn berries are dark liver-red.

Ginkgo biloba
Maidenhair tree
Height: to 18m

The maidenhair tree comes to us from prehistoric times, a unique species with no close living relatives. Although the leaves drop, it is more closely related to conifers than to other deciduous trees. The male tree is often preferred in a garden as it produces small pollen cones like hard catkins, while the female tree bears seeds that fall and give off an unpleasantly rancid stench.

The distinctive, fan-shaped, pale green leaves of this elegant tree turn bright golden in autumn before they fall. Trees usually start life slim and straight, but broaden to become wide and spreading as they mature. They like an open but sheltered position and in a warm climate ginkgos need regular water during heat waves, but are otherwise self-reliant. They will tolerate most soils but prefer them fairly rich and moist.

Laurus nobilis
Bay
Height: to 12m

Bay leaves crowned the Greek and Roman conquerors and champions – the term 'resting on your laurels' derives from this custom, referring to people who achieve but can't be bothered to repeat the effort. Apparently the Emperor Tiberius wore a bay-leaf wreath as insurance against lightning – surely reason enough to grow a bay tree!

This is a tree for every garden with its scented evergreen leaves for the kitchen and small, cream flowers in late winter before black berries. It is versatile: the bay trees can be kept small, single-stemmed and trimmed into lollipops or other shapes, or allow a specimen to grow into a substantial tree. If the roots are disturbed, bay will freely sucker to form an attractive hedge.

Bays will grow happily in well-drained soil in most conditions including near-drought once they are established, but won't survive very cold or near-tropical areas. Grow in full sun and water well when young. In frost-prone climates either grow a specimen in a pot and move it into shelter in winter, or consider wrapping a tree in frostproof material for protection.

Liriodendron tulipifera
Tulip tree
Height: to 25m

I debated this choice endlessly but the tulip tree is a tall and striking, dense, pyramidal-shaped tree for the larger garden, a highly desirable specimen tree for a temperate climate. It is grown for its glossy, light green, saddle shaped leaves that turn brilliant yellows and reds in autumn before they drop, and for its greenish-yellow spring flowers, shaped rather like tulips. I've grown tulip trees in Australia, where they will survive long, dry spells if protected by windbreaks, but they are not ideal for very hot, drought-prone areas, preferring a deep-moist soil. They produce the best autumn colour in the coolest conditions.

Magnolia grandiflora

Height: to 30m

You'll struggle to find a more magnificent tree than *Magnolia grandiflora*. With huge, glossy, green leaves backed bronze, and fragrant, creamy white flowers the shape of goblets and the size of porridge bowls in late summer. These beautiful evergreen trees thrive from the sub-tropics to cool temperate climates, but where winter is cold they like to be planted against a warm wall, although partial shade is also acceptable. They aren't fussy about water when they mature and, unlike many other magnolias, they are perfectly tolerant of alkaline as well as acidic soil, enriched with plenty of compost. I think their only downside is the way their huge leaves drop randomly, so large they demand to be swept up immediately.

This massive evergreen tree was once only for larger gardens, but more manageable varieties are now widely available with the same lovely lemon-scented flowers, albeit a trifle smaller.

M. grandiflora 'Little Gem' is a dwarf form growing no more than 5m tall, forming a loosely columnar tree.

M. grandiflora 'Saint Mary' is just as compact and flowers equally well – an ideal choice for a freestanding specimen as it forms a tidy dense tree, and responds well to winter pruning to shape it.

Malus spp.

Crab apple

Height: to 6m

When *Malus floribunda*'s cherry-pink buds open into small, white flowers, this means that spring has really arrived. This is an ideal garden tree, 6m high and wide, casting summer shade dense enough to sit beneath. I have also grown two favoured small crab apple trees, M. 'Golden Hornet' with springtime white blossom and really golden fruit in autumn lasting till winter arrives, and M. 'John Downie', again, decked in spring's white blossom with fruits a striking orange and red. M. 'Gorgeous' is a New Zealand introduction that is not well known in northern Europe, but it is true to its name with the most brilliant, large crabs. Then I am totally besotted with M. 'Evereste', clouded in spring in superb blossom, its crabs quite small and unassuming. I grow them to make cloud trees: three tall stems are angled out from the same hole and the branches trained to knit together. Crab apples prosper in both my Australian and English gardens, even by gravel paths, never needing as much attention as the cherries. They were mulched occasionally and watered only if they showed signs of wilting, with pruning minimal. In England they grow in one of the dampest areas and still flower each spring; they have been espaliered, which they respond to well to make the most fanciful, stylised shapes.

Nyssa sylvatica

Black gum/Black tupelo

Height: to 20m

Another wonderful specimen tree, broadly pyramidal in shape, with horizontal branches. I grow nyssa for its outstanding autumn foliage as its leaves turn from orange through to vivid bright red with lines of colour descending through the tree like ribbons. At Kennerton Green the nyssa grew against a row of tall, dark conifers that created a perfect background foil for its brilliance. The flower is insignificant, followed by a blackish, small fruit. Standard advice is to give the nyssa a sunny spot in damp, swampy soil, and mine at West Green House grows beside the lake with its roots, I'm sure, now nudging the water. But at Kennerton Green the tree had to fight for what water it received as the mighty conifers behind took more than their share of moisture. It survived temperatures above 30°C (86°F) with limited watering, so it definitely qualifies as resilient. Slow-growing, but worth the wait.

Prunus spp.
Japanese Flowering Cherry
Height: to 20m

Ornamental blossom trees, like the *Prunus* spp., originating in cooler climates will grow and flower in a wide range of temperatures if they are given sensible nurture. Wherever the Japanese cherry blossoms en masse there are tourists to marvel at its small powder-puff flower in bunches so dense it can block out the sky from beneath the tree.

There are many varieties and the name that says 'flowering cherry' to me is P. 'Kanzan', the variety with the fluffiest, double pink flowers on a tree that can grow to 20m high and nearly as wide. Just as sensational is P. 'Taihaku', the great white cherry, 8m of pure white blossom appearing just as new, shiny, bronze leaves emerge. These trees grow well in disparate climates. Driving into London past Richmond, I see a row of these trees established beside the road and in spring they are so splendid the appalling traffic becomes unimportant. These must be resilient trees to survive in this open windswept position, enduring the most intense and continuous car exhaust fumes. In Australia they grew on a steep bank beside a road, where all water drained away, and still they flourished.

The smaller Japanese cherry trees are pleasing choices for the town garden. P. 'Ukon', known as the green Japanese cherry, has been for me a rather spindly tree with clusters of unusual greenish-yellow flowers. P. 'Kiku-shidare-zakura' weeps from a slender trunk with double, deep pink flowers and P. 'Amanogawa' forms a 6m columnar and fragrant sentinel of semi-pink blossom, striking when planted to form a miniature grove. P. serrula is grown for its polished mahogany trunk, again a small tree with a spreading canopy of smaller, white flowers.

All prunus trees do need some attention, mulch, water in dry spells and a prune when the boughs become too heavy. However, there was in our line of blossom trees one long, low branch held firm by two prongs of a wooden fork. I felt it looked romantic in any season, but at flowering time it was a curve of pink froth just perfect for a heroine to be found sitting in.

Pyrus salicifolia var *orientalis* 'Pendula'
Weeping silver pear
Height: to 5m

The deciduous silver pear is one of the most elegant small trees with its fine, long, slender, silver-grey leaves and attractive form. It is excellent as a standard in a pot, as a single specimen, or even in a small avenue. I like to complement it by underplanting a summer ground covering of silver snow, *Cerastium tomentosum*, that is covered with white flowers above tiny, silver leaves and acts as an excellent weed suppressor.

Silver pears have grown happily for me in Australia and the UK in different soils but both with good drainage, however they do not like to dry out completely. In the warmth of southern New South Wales, facing the western sun on a perpetually dry slope, they were watered in extreme heat. In the UK a line of trees grows on an embankment between two streams of water. Silver pears prefer the sun or dappled shade, and in time their heads need trimming or they may appear to get too heavy for the slender trunk.

Quercus spp.
Oak
Height: to 35m

Oak trees are synonymous with age and stability. The fine stands beyond West Green House's front gates were planted to celebrate the victory at Waterloo in 1815 and still dominate the woodlands and the fields beyond.

Quercus robur, the English or pedunculate oak, is typically at least 25m tall and spreads as wide, a monumental tree with distinctive, dark green leaves and plentiful acorns. Homesick 19th-century British gardeners planted and tended these oaks in warmer climates and specimens are still flourishing in many dusty, hot towns in Australia around dry cricket grounds and as street trees. Oaks prefer rich planting soil, and reasonable moisture, but they are remarkably tolerant when mature. If you are short of space but still want oak, they can be grown as part of a hedge or pollarded.

Q. ilex, the evergreen Holm oak, is a naturally resilient form, found all around its native Mediterranean. Its leaves are a dull leathery green with silvery undersides and it produces bunches of long, creamy-grey catkins. I have grown these trees in a dry area in southern New South Wales, then beside the sea, and now in a moist, cool temperate garden in the UK. They like any soil except chalk and make excellent specimen trees and may be clipped into good solid hedges.

Q. cerris, the Turkey oak, is native to southern Europe and Asia, another monumental deciduous tree with paler leaves than the English oak. It is happy in a wide range of climates including coastal positions and alkaline soils, and is good as a specimen or as part of a mixed woodland planting.

Salix spp.
Willow
Height: various

The iconic image of a willow tree is perhaps the classical Chinese drawing of a large weeping tree hanging gracefully over a bridge, but there are also smaller decorative forms. I've classified them as resilient as they grow in the cold damp of England and heat-scorched areas of Australia, however most like to put their roots into dampness. *Salix caprea* 'Kilmarnock' may be an exception. It is a top-grafted small weeping tree growing to 2.5m; I planted one in a boggy area and had to move it to a drier spot. Willow trees can grow from cool regions into the sub-tropics in any type of soil, but are happiest with moisture in the sub-soil. Their roots can invade, so take advice before planting in a confined area, or close to housing.

S. caprea is the classic pussy willow or goat willow, with a mass of soft silvery-yellow catkins in spring, and slightly felty, grey-green leaves on swift-growing trees 6–10m tall.

S. babylonica var. *pekinensis* 'Tortuosa', the corkscrew willow, grows more slowly to 8m with curly branches like long, contorted fingers, making particularly dramatic outlines against a winter sky after the leaves have fallen. Its soft green-grey leaves are long and thin, but the main feature is the twisted stems, very architectural and of course wonderful for cutting. *S. sepulcralis* 'Chrysocoma' is the common hybrid weeping willow, growing to 15m in height and spreading with invasive roots, so definitely not one for small gardens.

Buddleja spp.
Butterfly bush/buddleia
Height: 2–4m

Among the most uncomplaining of plants, I have seen buddleias grow in the toughest of spots, such as along harsh embankments of railway lines. They flower from midsummer into autumn with long panicles of white, cream, yellow, pink, mauve, blue or purple flowers, sometimes scented, on arching branches of grey, felty leaves. Often covered with butterflies which love their nectar-rich flowers, buddleias will grow anywhere as long as they get sun, but some varieties become very wild and need drastic haircuts when flowering finishes in autumn. Most are extremely hardy and tolerant of any soil and lack of regular water.

Buddleja 'Lochinch' is an old, heavily scented, violet-blue garden hybrid that grows successfully into a small tree from Scotland to the Australian wheat plains.

B. davidii 'Black Knight' has the longest, dark violet, almost black, tresses on arching branches. Mine at West Green gives a too-sweet border the oomph it needs.

Ceanothus spp.
Height: various

This enthralling blue plant, which I think has the looks of a super star, is a star performer for the warmer garden, but I know many north European gardeners will take me to task for even considering this plant as being resilient. However I do find one variety *Ceanothus* 'Glorie de Versailles' grows successfully in the two gardens I have planted. When fully grown, this is a very large shrub of 2m, covered in powder-blue flowers in long panicles.

Both the plants are in full sun and well-drained, but I am told the reason this plant is so resilient is that it is a French 19th-century hybrid developed from an American east-coast parent and differs from the Californian species as it flowers from midsummer with spot flowers in autumn.

One ceanothus that friends with gardens in both cool and warm climates tell me I must have is C. 'Blue Cushion', an exceptional plant

that is really amicable. Only 90cm in height, it makes low cushions of intense blue withstanding heat and, I'm told, the cold climate of England's midlands.

Chaenomeles japonica
Ornamental/Japanese quince
Height: to 2m

In the depth of midwinter the formless collection of deep brown, thorny branches that is Japanese quince appears completely uninspiring. In fact, an informal quince hedge looks like a gardener's mistake. But just before the cold breaks it bursts into flower in thrilling red, peach, pink or white blossoms as the first glamorous treat of spring. It then retreats into obscurity with dull green leaves, but by autumn small, quince-shaped fruit form, often in profusion.

This plant is a survivor. It grows anywhere, never needs water, loves sun but copes with a minimum, and it is tolerant of frost and windy sites. And if you need to keep out sheep or any unwanted intruder it is an excellent barricade as its thorny branches grow at all angles and a few together make a natural fence.

Choisya ternata
Mexican orange blossom
Height: to 2.5m

Although this is only borderline resilient, if there is a protected site in sun or part shade, this dense evergreen has a place in your garden. Scented, star-shaped, white flowers appear in late spring through glossy, aromatic, dark green leaves – a glamorous and lovely foil for silvery or purple foliage plants. When protected from severest frost and wind, choisya will survive a chilly winter, but the leaves may yellow and take some time to revive the following year. But for the warmer garden it is a must.

Hydrangea quercifolia
Oakleaf hydrangea
Height: to 2.5m

A very desirable and tolerant plant. Its leaves are large, elegant oakleaves, dull green and bronzed backdrops for long panicles of flowers that begin pure white at midsummer. The flowers gradually turn from white to green into pink to complement the striking, reddish bronze of the leaves in autumn before they fall.

This hydrangea grew for me in Australia along a long, well-drained terrace edge, alternating from full sun to shade, and in Hampshire it is in dappled shade beside a stream. It must be the cross-over super star, a uniquely tolerant hydrangea, while other members of its family need rich soil, plentiful water and protection.

Cistus spp.
Rock rose
Height: 1–2.5m

With grey-green evergreen leaves and petals like fine silk, these fragile-looking and well-behaved shrubs are so resilient they always amaze me. As with many plants from the warm, dry areas around the Mediterranean, they are happy in stony, dry soil, but will die if they sit in the cold with wet feet. Most are fully hardy through most of the UK and will be harmed only by exceptionally wet and cold winters. Their most important requirements are full sun and excellent drainage. They are perfectly suitable for seaside planting and windy areas, and few other plants will happily tolerate equally rough and dry conditions while continuing to flower for months.

Cistus come in many shapes and sizes, from dwarf and compact to large, upright shrubs, others prostrate and spreading. Their open, rose-like flowers may be white or all shades of pink, often with deep blotches and prominent stamens. There is a cistus for everyone, some are hardier than others, so check when you buy.

Cistus salviifolius 'Prostratus' is a lovely, white, ground-hugging form for a warm garden. C.x lusitanicus 'Decumbens' has the same qualities but is hardier. The flowers come and go quickly; however as they flower profusely, you'll scarcely notice.

C. laurifolius is the hardiest white-flowered spreading form; C. 'Grayswood' the hardiest pale pink; C. oblongifolius is a very vigorous hardy upright form.

Hebe spp.
Height: to 2m

In this large hardy species of deciduous and evergreen shrubs of varying sizes, there are varieties of hebes suitable for a wide climate range. In drought-prone areas the most common forms are evergreen with long, violet-blue flowers above shiny, deep green leaves. Hebe x franciscana, which grows to around 1.2m, is super tolerant; there's an old and tough specimen at Kennerton Green that weathers drought, cold and intermittent watering without blinking. Most hebes will thrive in full sun or dappled shade with a good spring mulch on a well-drained soil. Mine has survived frosts but horticultural gurus say it can be tender. Tough hebes work especially well as hedges in warmer coastal areas.

H. albicans is a superbly hardy evergreen, no more than 60cm tall, producing a cloud of white flowers above glaucous, silvery-green leaves in midsummer. When the garden is looking tired it is softly beautiful. Mine likes its sheltered position on gravelly soil in a small walled garden at West Green House where it is mulched perhaps once every two years.

Pyracantha spp.
Firethorn
Height: to 6m

Thorny pyracanthas are often grown beside roadsides as informal windbreaks making excellent deterrents. Evergreen, and covered in tiny, white flowers in spring, they are tough and versatile, but the main reason to grow them is for their brilliant, shiny berries in autumn. They tolerate most soils, and establish quickly in well-drained conditions. They can be left alone without any maintenance, though in some situations they may need regular pruning to keep them under control and thick gloves are always needed. The 'Saphyr' range is resilient to fire blight and other fungal diseases, so is most suitable for warmer areas. *Pyracantha* 'Orange Glow' has orange berries, P. 'Saphyr Jaune' is a yellow form, P. 'Saphyr Rouge' is red. All grow to around 3m height and spread.

Ribes sanguineum
Flowering currant
Height: to 3m

At that moment when winter never seems to end, the bright pink, tubular bell flowers of flowering currants appear cheerfully hanging in bunches from the greyish-green branches. It is a plant for many climates: we had a strong hedge in Australia where the rainfall was 58cm annually and it grows in a friend's garden in Stockholm, facing a sea that freezes in winter.

Flowering currants are rather untidy, upright deciduous shrubs. The pink ones are classic English country-garden plants, appearing in almost every cottage hedge, and they are best planted in a mixed hedge for their early cheer. Don't be tempted to pick them for the house or you'll be wondering if a neighbouring cat has been inside marking his territory. *Ribes sanguinem* 'King Edward VII' has crimson flowers; 'White Icicle' has large white blooms.

Rosmarinus spp.
Rosemary
Height: various

Everyone knows rosemary, the greyish-green evergreen shrub covered in fine, aromatic, needle-like leaves and clusters of tiny flowers in shades of blue, mauve or white. One of the most succulent meals I can ever remember was a slice of pancetta rolled around what looked like half a hedge of rosemary, roasted and sliced and sold by the roadside in a village north of Rome. The aroma of the rosemary lived on in my taste buds and since then rosemary has become the most important of my kitchen herbs. It grows in any soil and by the sea, but there must be drainage and full sun. Rosemary is usually hardy, even through cold winters, but plants have a tendency to shuffle off without much warning, so always keep some young ones in waiting – cuttings take easily.

I have planted a hedge of *Rosmarinus officinalis* 'Miss Jessopp's Upright' wherever I have lived. It has proved a tough stalwart, but I'm told R. *officinalis* 'Gorizia' is even hardier.

Briza maxima
Great quaking grass
Height: 60cm

A quite substantial, gravelly hill rose up behind my family home, covered in the native eucalyptus that grew in close stands above a carpet of briza with lantern-like seedheads. This annual grass was introduced to Australia and quickly colonised among the wildflowers on poor soil to create a natural advertisement for a perfect grass for a wildflower planting. Its papery seedheads nod from fine arched stems and rustle in the slightest breeze.

Easy to grow and hardy, quaking grass accepts any soil, sun or dappled shade. If given a too comfortable a home, it can self-seed to become an invasive weed in borders, but in colder or more extreme climates it makes an ideal accompaniment, peeping through perennials. It's much appreciated by flower arrangers.

Calamagrostis x acutiflora 'Karl Foerster'
Feather reed grass
Height: 1.8m

An überfashionable, tall, upright grass. It begins the year as a stand of pale green stems, it flowers in a misty haze in summer, then deepens to a rusty brown, holding its colour and vertical shape all winter until it is cut down for the cycle to begin again. Highly architectural in the autumn and winter garden, this is an easy grass, accepting full sun or part shade, lashing rain or hot sun. Plants subdivide easily to be replanted in late autumn or spring.

Elymus magellanicus
Blue wheat grass
Height: 50cm

When I was planning the garden for the Villa Cristina by the sea, I read about this blue, blue grass recommended for coastal gardens and felt I must try it. Now it is also being planted at West Green House, supplied by a local grower, so I think I have found another superb blue grass that is truly resilient. It forms a perfectly rounded tussock of silvery blue, with gently pointed leaves. Plants produce bluish-purple flowerheads in summer that fade to a biscuit colour as they mature, something I'm looking forward to. Although I am told the grass copes with any well-drained soils, I've placed mine on a gravelled soil in full sun on the open terrace in Majorca, unprotected from the sea. At West Green it is in a low, dry bed. Apparently it thrives on neglect in hot, dry spots, liking gravel gardens, but it will not cope with excessive winter wet.

Festuca glauca
Blue fescue grass
Height: 30cm

An impossibly electric-blue, hardy, little grass that grows in neat clumps and also produces spikes of blue-green flowers in midsummer, but these tend to be rather insignificant so are best removed to keep the clumps well shaped. I grow the very dwarf *Festuca glauca* 'Blaufuchs' which makes a superb 15cm (6in) tussock as an edging to the path in the West Green House vegetable garden.

Fescue must have a well-drained soil and a sunny spot, and plants can get a bit tatty-looking after long, hot periods, but most of the time they are so attractive and vivid they are absolutely worth growing. Comb through the plants in winter to remove dead foliage and divide regularly to keep them tidy.

Lagurus ovatus
Hare's tail grass
Height: 45cm

Hare's tail is a much-loved, small annual grass with dense, fluffy flowerheads that look so silky they just beg to be stroked. It adds a gentle softness to a border or a small plant grouping. The flowerheads start pale green in spring, turn cream in summer and bleach to a pale brown in autumn above silvery-green foliage.

In warm climates this grass will self-seed to cover gravelly soil quickly, relishing full sun and any rain, so cut the drying seedheads back in autumn to prevent it becoming invasive. In cooler conditions sow an entire seedhead in a pot, then transplant the seedlings. Hare's tail is rarely invasive in cooler gardens, but in the warmer parts of southern England the plants can naturalise.

Panicum virgatum 'Rehbraun'
Red prairie switch grass
Height: 1.2m

This wonderful hardy, evergreen grass ages to a rich, burnt red-purple in autumn, when the fine stems hold aloft a reddish haze of tiny dots of flowers. The grass catches every breeze and moves continuously; it's both sturdy and diaphanous. For full effect, this grass needs mass grouping, when all the tiny plumes resemble a cloud of insects. I have planted it by a strong blue stand of asters, then tickling the chin of *Eupatorium maculatum* 'Purple Bush', a most companionable planting. Switch is tough, coping with any soils, surviving sun, wind, cold and snow. Cut back at autumn's end or in early spring.

Miscanthus sinensis
Maiden grass/Chinese silver grass and others
Height: from 70cm to 2.7m

Miscanthus offers a superb range of many magical tall grasses for the autumn border. All have reed-like stems, often subtly coloured, and many have interesting foliage. In late summer their height increases with their plumed flowerheads, arching panicles of silky-haired spikes. The longer and hotter the summer, the more profuse the flowering. Do check the variety you buy, for most are of monstrous size and even a dwarf variety will grow over 1m. The plants are easy to grow and hardy and seem to survive any soil, sun, shade, warmth and cold, but if they're too well cared for they become out of hand and are hard work to control. Thin them out and cut back annually in spring.

Miscanthus sinensis 'Cabaret' grows to 2.4m; the leaves have white centres and dark green margins. The leaves of similarly sized *M. sinensis* 'Cosmopolitan' have dark green centres with creamy white margins. Slightly smaller at 1.5m, *M. sinensis* 'Variegatus' has narrow, stripy green and white

leaves. All have buff to pink flowerheads. *M. sinensis* 'Ferner Osten' grows to 2m with large, purplish-red flower spikes fading to silvery buff. Unusual yellow-green stems stay prominent through winter, with sparse foliage. *M. sinensis* 'Flamingo' reaches 1.5m; a favourite for its delicate, pale green foliage with extra-long arching flower stems and silky, pale purple-pink plumes in late summer. I first saw clumps of *M. sinensis* 'Zebrinus', Zebra grass, a spectacular 2m green grass banded by cream rings, growing in San Francisco as a specimen in a lawn. The gardener told me she thought it splendid, but she couldn't find a suitable home for it. I've found it just as difficult to place in a border, but beside a pool it looks marvellous. It will need some water but seems perfectly hardy. *M. sinensis* 'Strictus', Porcupine grass, at 1m, is a lower form of zebra grass, and easier to place. Spiky foliage is marked with horizontal cream-yellow banding across the leaves, autumn flowerheads are pinkish.

Alcea rosea
Hollyhock
Height: 1–3.5m

Twice hollyhocks have stopped me in my stride, once beside a stone wall in Norfolk, hundreds of them swaying in the sea breeze, the others growing in sand-filled beds beside the Aswan Dam in upper Egypt. They are biennial rather than annual, but treat them like annuals. Stiff stems can grow to a towering 3.5m with the large, saucer-like flowers blooming up most of the stem, complemented by rough, furry leaves. The silky, chocolate-maroon *Alcea rosea* 'Nigra' is hugely fashionable, as is the fully double *A. rosea* 'Peaches and Cream' whose spires of fluffy powder-puff flowers are soft peach with a hint of pink. Hollyhocks in ideal conditions will self-seed, but do not like over-rich soil and need space and air. Totally drought-resistant, they do not appreciate over-watering, and tend to suffer from rust in humid conditions. Once their flowering period is over, either cut down or pull out the spent plant and collect or scatter the seeds.

Amaranthus spp.
Amaranth
Height: to 1.2m

A traditional food plant in parts of Asia and the Americas, amaranth is known to most of us as a leafy green vegetable or, more commonly, as an ornamental annual for late summer. *Amaranthus caudatus* is the traditional grain-producing form, while *A. caudatus* 'Fat Spike' is an extraordinary annual with huge, velvety, ruby or yellowish-green tassels falling from a stem of over a metre. It's definitely not a plant for everybody: the plumes are reptilian to some and joyous to others. It is a daring self-seeder. *A. paniculatus* has huge, fluffy plumes like an over-exotic grass; it includes forms with dramatic dark foliage and claret feathers, others golden and bright red. *A. tricolor* needs more prolonged sun, so does less well in cooler climates, but otherwise amaranths will handle all conditions except long, damp summers.

Calendula officinalis
Pot marigold
Height: 45–60cm

Calendulas resemble multi-layered daisies, traditionally with a ruff of golden-orange petals around a prominent eye. Grown for centuries as medicinal plants, they are cheerful and prolific flowers. There are single and double forms, in colours from pale apricot through sunset shades to deep bronze.

I currently favour *Calendula officinalis* 'Touch of Red', a mixture accurately described as looking antique. Calendula is a good grower which self-seeds easily – too easily in some cases – but it's simple to pull out if it falls where you don't want it.

Cerinthe

Height: to 60cm

I often think of a peacock when I look at the deep aqua-blue leaves and branches of the cerinthe, for there in the bracts are purples with deeper green, the colours of the eye of a peacock feather. This plant has survived and flourished for me in both warm and cool temperate climates, standing 60cm tall by late summer and often self-seeding to reappear next year.

Sow in cooler climates in the greenhouse and plant out once the soil is warmer. This strong plant has small, tubular flowers that appear darkest blue with a mix of maroon highlighted by yellow. A compact form, *Cerinthe minor* 'Bouquet Gold', is recommended for containers.

Cleome
Spider flower
Height: to 1m

Tall, filmy and unusual, the spider flower is a must-have in a full late summer border as its airy form lightens any block of flowering plants. Pink, purple or white flowers resemble long-legged insects on top of their long stems. They're best placed in a mass border planting as their lower leaves become shabby as they grow and need to be hidden.

Raise cleome seedlings indoors in cool climates, and plant out well after threats of frost. The plants are very tolerant of heat and comparative drought and flowering freely from late summer well into autumn.

Cosmos spp.

Central and South America, South Africa

Height: to 2m

Driving north of Cape Town, I saw giant swathes of cosmos nearly hiding the country road. It was remarkable – the entire landscape was lost under the softly moving, daisy-style flowers held high on the slenderest of stems that gently swayed in the breeze.

Many of us know the 1.2m stems holding bright daisies in colours from white to all shades of pink, backed by fine ferny foliage. But this is only part of the story: cosmos can be every shade of an orange sunset, from tall, leggy creatures to shrubby 30cm forms. *Cosmos sulphureus* 'Lemon Bird' is a sharp golden citrus, *C. bipinnatus* 'Pied Piper Red' and other bicolours are delightful, and forms with fluted petals, usually sold as C. 'Seashells', are charming. There are also forms with ragged-edged petals and fluffy doubles.

Sow cosmos indoors in cooler climates and plant them out from early summer to flower from summer into autumn. Sun-loving, they thrive in a regularly prepared bed, with average water, but can be super-understanding if the water is limited. In their ideal warmer climate they will self-seed.

Eschscholzia californica

California poppy

Height: to 30cm

A native of the western US the bright orange-gold California poppy has a characteristic four-petalled flower, which opens above lacy, blue-green foliage. There are also rosy red, yellow and creamy forms. In a warm garden this is a perennial, elsewhere a self-seeding annual, that is drought- and frost-tolerant and useful to cover rough and sandy soils, flowering in midsummer.

Lathyrus odorata

Sweet pea

Height: to 2.5m

The charm and fragrance of sweet peas is definitely one of God's gifts, but although they are generally a reliable annual with prolific flowers, if the season is just too dark and cold they may sulk, refusing to perform without sun.

Sow seeds indoors and plant seedlings into well-mulched beds, giving them plenty of water to start. Tie the plants into a frame, or onto a tripod or canes, as they continue growing throughout the summer season, and keep picking the flowers to ensure the longest flowering period. Ideally, plant one lot of seedlings as soon as the ground begins to warm, another a few weeks later, and many gardeners manage a third sowing to keep them flowering through September, but they do not like very hot weather in their early stages. As soon as plants become ragged and brown remove them and allow a companion climber, perhaps a bean, to take over and fill the gap.

Sweet peas come in hues from almost black to brightest white with most colours in between, including many bicolours and some with petals outlined in another colour. *Lathyrus grandiflora* 'Matucana' is a 2m climber said to have been introduced into Britain 300 years ago and remains one of the most beautiful in the garden, two-tone purple with an intensely strong scent.

Papaver spp.
Annual poppy
Height: to 30cm

One year I fell in love with the annual *Papaver somniferum* (Paeoniiflorum Group) 'Black Paeony' and planted a whole bed of this negligée-black ball of ruffles. Standing quietly in the garden, I would hear the continual sound of the poppy buds bursting open, small 'pops' as the flowers unfolded. Shirley poppies, *Papaver rhoeas*, are also worth considering, cultivars of the original bright red corn poppies. These are now available in a wide range of colours from brightest scarlet to softest pink, with many bicolours, and single and double forms. Slightly lax and straggly *P. commutatum* 'Ladybird'

is another field poppy relative, a single ruby bloom blotched black that seems to belong among the vegetables. It grows 45cm tall and accepts what soil it finds. These annual poppies all grow happily from seed, scattered in either autumn or spring. Once you have them in your garden they are likely to stay. Among the border's earliest flowers are the papery Iceland poppies, *P. nudicaule*, cups of cool orange, cream, yellows and whites, held on stiff, furry stems as spring arrives. Instead of sowing these from seed, raise seedlings indoors and plant them out.

Tagetes spp.
Marigold
Height: 20–90cm

Tagetes bring with them the image of hot countries. They have spread from their native Americas throughout almost every hot climate, and are equally happy planted in cool temperate gardens for a fiery summer display. I have both tagetes, calendulas and pot marigolds, running through the vegetable gardens at West Green House.

Tagetes spp. are erect, with ferny, small leaves and round heads of tidy, very ruffled petals, some growing to 90cm, others dwarf and compact to 30cm. They are usually sunny shades of oranges and yellows through to cream, some with maroon or bronze highlights, all with their own particular musky odour. Each year I grow the creamy, erect *Tagetes* 'French Vanilla', 35cm tall, a chic garden addition.

It takes an extremely hot day for a marigold to wilt – they are exceptional annuals, adapted to a wide range of climates. If deadheaded regularly, they will flower all summer and autumn until the frosts come.

Achillea millefolium
Yarrow
Height: 30cm–1m

A blue-grey mat of softly aromatic yarrow foliage is an inviting ground cover for any garden, thriving in the most dry and difficult conditions to throw up stiff stems each holding a generous umbel of tiny clusters of flowers. Yarrow will even colonise a stone wall, but also thrives in moist sunny or partly shaded soils. In drier gardens it is a beautifully behaved plant, but given too many luxuries of mulch, water and sun it can become invasive. A first-year-flowering perennial, its early summer flowers should be cut back as they fade and plants should be subdivided in cooler months.

Yarrow blooms in shades of white, cream, pink, yellow, copper and oranges. I like the terracotta tones of *Achillea* 'Paprika' and *A.* 'Walther Funcke' to highlight flowers of blue or gold.

Agapanthus spp.
African lily
Height: 30cm–1.2m

In Australia, New Zealand, the Mediterranean and its native South Africa, agapanthus is tough, but in England it has always been considered frost-tender, although some new introductions do seem to be resilient. The species includes towering giants over 1m tall down to tiny *Agapanthus* 'Tinkerbell', 30cm of pale blue flowers above regency striped white and green leaves. The evergreen *A.* 'Purple Cloud' is a superb plant recommended for a wide climate range, but I subscribe to the rule of thumb that evergreen agapanthus prefer the warmer zones, while the deciduous varieties, such as the *A. campanulatus* group, seem truly hardy.

Agapanthus must have full sun and well-drained soil; even in the hottest areas they will not flower in shade. They are exemplary pot plants as their water requirements are minimal and they keep smart and tidy in the most trying conditions, making them superb plants for warm-climate holiday homes. In the cooler zones I have found the smaller deciduous varieties have coped with the cold, with a layer of mulch as a winter blanket. In ideal climates agapanthus multiply quickly and every other year it is wise to check and subdivide as necessary in spring.

Aquilegia spp.
Columbine/granny's bonnet
Height: 30–90cm

As early spring bulbs fade and tulip leaves become ragged, columbines or granny's bonnets return in profusion, with bobbing, ephemeral flowers on fine, stiff stems. The traditional blues and slightly murky pinks are joined by newer varieties in a huge range of colours including many bicolours, with single, double or deeply ruffled flowers. Some feature long tails known as spurs in intriguing shades. Self-sown seedlings are not often true to form and may appear in unexpected colours, but some of the older forms will reproduce accurately, and there are many new named hybrids in a smart collection of colours.

Deep purple forms are pure black magic and add drama to sweet pale spring borders. *Aquilegia vulgaris* var. *stellata* 'Black Barlow' is a tight-flowered, old double form that comes true to seed, pure ink. *A.* 'William Guiness' has black and white flowers; *A.* 'Roman Bronze' has black-bronze flowers with extraordinary golden-yellow foliage. Most are very easy to grow either from seed or bought as established plants. Wherever I've planted them they have accepted rain, drought, early frosts, sun and dappled shade. Cut them back after flowering and they simply disappear, usually to reappear in spring. They do not like to be over-watered and can develop a white mildew or rot. I particularly like them for a woodland edge, a dreamy sight naturalised in drifts under newly emerging leaves.

Chrysanthemum spp.

Height: 30cm–1.5m

This flower was so revered in Oriental cultures that the term 'The Chrysanthemum Throne' still represents the authority of the Emperor of Japan. In Chinese art it is the symbol of autumn, having been grown in China since the 15th century BC. Today it is popular with garden societies throughout the world.

Chrysanthemums are broadly broken into two groups: hardy garden chrysanths are perennials that can be overwintered in the ground through most northern latitudes, while exhibition forms are tender and require special treatment. The many garden forms are categorised by the shape of their petals, including pompons, incurving balls, quills and spiders. Some have blooms the size of little buttons, some huge saucers. I'm susceptible to the sherbet-green spider *Chrysanthemum* 'Shamrock' and the dark mahogany-red C. 'Duchess of Edinburgh', but the pompom-shaped flowers and the cushions of tiny blooms of C. *indicum* 'Early Charm' always find a home with me.

Chrysanthemums can bloom from summer far into autumn until cut back by frosts. They grow from root cuttings planted in early summer into a well-mulched and well-drained bed, with space for air to circulate. They accept heat and dry spells in a wide climate range, but do not like prolonged drought. To get the best show, pinch out the tips where the bud will form to encourage a bushier plant and more blooms. Regular deadheading keeps the show going for many by cutting back to the ground to overwinter. The list of these flowers goes on and on, but in the warm inland garden I knew as a child the early spray varieties grew well. Today I plant white forms from the Margaret Collection and a September-flowering pompon 'Red Bronze'.

Armeria spp.

Thrift

Height: 25–50cm

Sea thrift, *Armeria maritima*, is an ideal tough little candidate for dry areas, forming grass-like clumps with dozens of papery, bobbing, drumstick heads in pinks or whites. Delightful lining paths, it has formed front-of-the-border groups for me in both warm and cool gardens as it is impervious to drought, sun, cold winters and low light, and it flowers from spring for many months. The one priority is that it must have excellent drainage otherwise it will rot, and it may need an occasional water in prolonged heat. *A. leucocephala* 'Corsica', taller and more reddish than *A. maritima*, is said to be most tolerant of heat. As groups become too large subdivide them, clear out old leaves and replant.

perennials

Convallaria majalis
Lily of the valley
Height: 30cm

Celebrated throughout history for its fragrance and beauty, lily of the valley carries small, arching stems of highly scented white bells surrounded by cool green leaves in late spring to create memorable ground cover.

Standard advice is to plant lily of the valley in autumn in leafy humus, typically in the dappled shade of deciduous trees. As the plant matures the rhizomes spread to form a mat of roots underground and produce a carpet of flowers in spring. But I have seen wonderful shows of these little flowers growing in drought-prone central Victoria, and from pure clay in New South Wales, and proving resilient in acid soils in sun with just a weekly water, so this fragile-seeming flower is tougher than it looks. The giant variety, *Convallaria majalis* 'Fortin's Giant', is less tough, but an inspiring inclusion in a warm garden.

Crocosmia spp.
Montbretia
Height: 60cm–1.2m

Crocosmia is a very fashionable plant for a prairie-style garden, planted among autumn grasses, but I have them through a long drift of earlier spring-flowering *Iris sibirica*, giving me a bed of fine, tall leaves with different hues of flowers from one end of the year to the other, starting with blues and ending in reds and golds. Arching, sword-like leaves support long, thin stems of bell-shaped flowers in dashing colours from lemon to orange and fiery red, with *Crocosmia* 'Jackanapes' a striking two-toned red and yellow. I think the best red so far is 'Lucifer'; and 'Gerbe d'Or' a lovely golden yellow above bronze leaves. A good match for the taller grasses is the pale yellow 1.2m 'Paul's Best Yellow'.

In warm, moist conditions they can become invasive, but crocosmia are particularly good for drier gardens as they survive in harsh conditions with minimal water. Subdivide them in autumn or spring as clumps can quickly become too thick.

Dicentra spectabilis
Bleeding heart
Height: 25-60cm

I'm never sure which aspect of this plant is more beautiful, the deeply cut leaves or the stems of nodding, heart-shaped flowers. Although hailing from the woodlands of the northwest USA, bleeding heart has proved reliably hardy in areas subject to hot, dry summers, and is a regular in northern hemisphere gardens where it is untroubled by shade, direct sun or damp corners.

There is an excellent range of *Dicentra*, with a choice of leaf colour from steely blue to grey-green, light green and pewter, with flowers in deep red, pink, white, cream and bicolour. The blue-leafed and pink-flowered *Dicentra* 'King of Hearts' is compact and neatly covers the ground, flowering at around 25cm, whilst the locket-shaped, pink and white *D. spectabilis* grows to about 60cm, the stems arching well above the leaves with dozens of flowers forming to hang down from the tops.

Dianthus spp.
Pinks
Height: various

Among the huge dianthus family are garden pinks, sweet Williams and carnations. Perhaps the best known in the garden are the biennial *Dianthus barbatus* group, old-fashioned sweet Williams in shades of red, pink and cream, perfect for a border's edge. *D. barbatus* 'Sooty' is the deepest maroon to black form, growing to 40cm in full sun and a well-drained soil. It is happy in most conditions but dislikes persistent wet or continuous drought. Carnations, fragrant, stiff and long-lasting, are among the perennials in the dianthus family, also liking warmth, but they are less resilient and slightly fussy as they prefer to be staked and watered regularly with excess buds removed in order to produce a few perfect blooms.

The stars of the family must be the scented pinks bred with stripes, ringed eyes, ruffles and shaggy frills. There are striking varieties in white, all the pinks through to the deepest reds, with fragrance that beats anything you may find on the perfume counter. They are clump-forming, perfectly behaved, long-flowering plants that need minimum attention and many have attractive, silver-grey evergreen foliage to boot. They are impervious to the temperature gauge and deliciously fragrant with a characteristic sweet spicy scent. Deadhead and divide if required in late autumn but do provide all dianthus with well-drained soil as they'll sulk if overwatered.

D. 'Mrs Sinkins' is a classic Victorian cottage garden plant with shaggy, white flowers, evergreen silvery-blue leaves and a very heady fragrance. 'Doris' is light pink with a deep salmon eye, just 15cm tall. The clove-scented *D. caryophyllus* varieties include deepest red 'Eleanor's Old Irish', and ruby-red 'Fenbow Nutmeg' which has the strongest nutmeg/clove scent of all.

Dierama spp.
Angel's/fairy fishing rod
Height: to 1.2m

I first saw a large clump of angel's fishing rod when I was a tourist in England, its arching stems with pink bells bending over a fast-flowing stream in a Gloucestershire village. I was enraptured and thought, 'How English,' mentally placing them in the 'can't have' catalogue – until I was walking through my favourite nursery in central Victoria and there they were, growing superbly. They are resilient to heat and drought, their tall, arching flower stems bedecked with bell-shaped blooms above fine evergreen foliage. The fine branches of flowers bend and sway in the slightest breeze, so they need space to be seen.

Colours are pure white, pinks, lilac and inky shades and conventional advice is to give them moist soil and sun or shade. But I'd argue they are happiest in a sunny, dry garden where water just arrives when the heavens bring it. I've found that in the UK they like the gravelly dry spots near a path; if they're too well fed or watered they rot.

Echinacea spp.
Cone flower
Height: 20–50cm

This is an American prairie plant, forming a large daisy around a prominent cone on top of a strong stem with deep green leaves. It belongs to the 'in crowd' as a late-summer-into-autumn accompaniment to grasses, coming in shades of pink, orange and yellow with both green and white forms. Cut back after flowering and grow where there is full sun. Water as necessary.

Erigeron karvinskianus
Fleabane/Spanish daisy
Height: 20–50cm

This tiny, pink and white daisy was used inspiringly by early 20th-century garden designers such as Edna Walling, who softened her hard landscaped terraces with veils of erigeron. Up close the effect perhaps was not so memorable, but from the middle distance it was ethereal. The little daisy heads do seem to float on their wiry stems above the greenish-bronze foliage. *Erigeron glaucus* 'Seabreeze' is a short, lilac-pink form with a little more substance above evergreen foliage. It will grow anywhere, not only in beds, but also through cracks in paths or on dry stone walls, self-seeding with abandon. In these drier spaces it will withstand a northern hemisphere winter, but it is at home in sun, drought and in sand dunes. It does need controlling with a firm haircut in autumn; in fact I pull out my old plants, for it spreads on hairy roots that seem to reach into the farthest crevices.

Eupatorium maculatum atropurpureum
Joe Pye weed
Height: to 2m

This may be the supremely popular plant of the decade. I have yet to see a newly designed border without its heads of dusty purple flowers in late summer and autumn, towering on sturdy stems above the lance-shaped leaves. Some gardeners let the flower heads darken for winter, theatrical above the grass skeletons, to be cut right back when the new season garden is prepared, but I cut the plants down once flowering is over.

When planted in the temperate Northern hemisphere, where it originates, it will self-seed unless firmly controlled, surviving through wet, cold, dry and hot seasons as long as it has some air around it and good drainage. If there is the space, try planting this lofty perennial behind a pink-flowering miscanthus, perhaps *Miscanthus sinensis* 'Rotsilber', for supreme autumn colour.

Gaura lindheimerei
Butterfly plant
Height: 1–1.2m

The flowers of gaura appear to be floating on air like butterflies, fluttering above their fine, stiff stems, but its true value for me is that it blooms in the late summer, a delicately pretty plant to bridge the flowering gap at this time. Pink-and-white-flowered *Gaura lindheimeri* is the best known, a generously flowering, bushy plant for a garden's edge, perfect to veil plants past their best as summer begins to end. *G. lindheimerei* 'Crimson Butterflies' has reddish leaves and bright pink flowers. *G. lindheimerei* 'Siskiyou Pink' is a mass of mid-pink blooms and 'Whirling Butterflies' is a white selection.

Gaura has long tap roots to mine for any moisture and likes it quite tough. It prefers a hot, dry summer but will survive most conditions except prolonged wet, and does not always come through harsh northern winters. In cold areas wait until spring before cutting back the old growth.

Iris germanica
Bearded iris
Height: various

An enduring memory is seeing these tall, elegant, beautiful and resilient flowering plants, in profusion along a friend's hot and dusty drive near the city of Goulbourn in New South Wales, which had been in drought for four years. I have planted them in Hampshire, but they tend to rot in my low, damp soil except in truly hot summers. However, most UK gardeners grow them in fine displays, so they are definitely worthwhile.

The bearded iris is a handsome plant. The flowers, on erect stalks surrounded by greyish, sword-shaped leaves, bear a front petal falling forward from standard petals, decorated with either veins, dots, lines, ruffles or all of them. The colours are magnificent, plain and mixtures of almost every colour apart from red, and they come in sizes from standard to giant. Cut back the strong stalks after flowering, and as the leaves become unsightly take these back too. I've planted salvias around my iris plots as their flowers follow on in a mass to help cover the spent iris patches. To divide iris simply lift the corms in winter, break a few shoots away and replant.

Iris germanica needs a gritty, porous soil and in a cool climate the bulbs should be placed just below the surface of the soil to achieve maximum warmth. In dry areas this flower is uncomplaining and magnificent.

Knautia spp.
Field scabious
Height: 80cm–1.2m

Another plant that loves the company of grasses, knautia needs to be part of the crowd or it becomes little more than a collection of brilliant dots flowering from midsummer through till autumn. Knautia is easy to grow, happy in well-mulched beds or semi-wasteland embankments with an occasional watering. Stars of the family include *Knautia macedonica*, 80cm tall with double, wine-red flowers, and *K. macedonica* pink-flowered, the pale pink form. *K.* 'Jardin d'en Face' is 60cm tall with pale blue pincushion flowers.

Lavandula spp.
Lavender
Height: various

The inevitable Mediterranean image are rows of lavender in fields glowing purple in the bright light, but lavender is also an essential of the European cottage garden and a cherished survivor in dry gardens everywhere. Lavenders come in a huge range of varieties and sizes. The hardiest I've found is the traditional English lavender, *Lavandula angustifolia*, that is usually around 1.5m tall and performs as well in UK gardens as in drier areas. It is hardy and waterwise with long, beautiful spikes of flowers in lavender blues, pinks and whites. L. *angustifolia* likes porous, gravelly soil and happily tolerates alkaline sandy soils, so is a reliable choice for seaside gardens.

I am a huge fan of the violet-flowered and compact, 30cm-tall L. *angustifolia* 'Hidcote' which is reliable and easy, and of L. *a.* 'Munstead', another dwarf form but with flowers of lavender blue; there's also a white form. Fully hardy Dutch lavender, L. x *intermedia* 'Grosso', is taller at around 75cm with mid-blue flowers and tolerates more dampness. It is one of the best for hedging.

L. *stoechas*, the popular bunny's ear lavender, is attractive and aromatic but it becomes very scraggy in wet winters, although the colour combination of darkest purple L. *stoechas* 'Rocky Road', with ears of pale pink against the green is irresistible.

Lavenders strike easily from cuttings and a firm prune after flowering keeps them shapely. Although surprisingly resilient to cold winters, lavenders are sunlovers and must never be tucked away in cold corners or allowed to become waterlogged.

Lychnis coronaria
Rose campion
Height: to 80cm

Lychnis has the same effect as knautia in a grass border: dots of brilliant colour making pinpoints of coloured light amongst the vertical stems. Lychnis also forms an excellent matting ground cover for poor, dry areas; its silver-grey rosettes of leaves all but concealed a dry embankment for me at Kennerton Green, embellished with tiny, flat flowers in cerise or white above the fine, grey stems. It does get tatty at season's end, so is perhaps best in a mixed setting. It is a very hardy perennial that will grow in hot or cold climates, self-seeding freely and accepting the poorest of soil – as long as it is well-drained.

Nepeta spp.
Catmint
Height: 15–70cm

I'm convinced that every open garden I visit in the UK has at least one bed of nepeta underplanting roses. I'm guilty too, for it just works so well. Both flower around the same period with the nepeta skirting the awkward rose stems and its hazy bluish-mauve flowers complementing so many pinks, creams and whites.

Among many useful cultivars perhaps the best is bushy 45–70cm-tall, pale blue *Nepeta* 'Six Hills Giant' with classic, fine, light grey, aromatic leaves, or the 45cm deep violet *N. racemosa* 'Walker's Low' which repeat flowers if cut back after the first summer flowering. *N. racemosa* 'Little Titch' is a good dwarf form with lavender flowers just 15cm high.

Catmints like sun, cope with frost and tolerate drought but do prefer an occasional dose of water. After flowering cut them back to base and many will repeat. They need regular division and are among the easiest plants to propagate: break off a stem and it will easily root in water.

Papaver orientale
Oriental poppy
Height: to 2m

This is for me spring's most spectacular flower, robust, dominant, almost aggressive in its size and vividness. Most produce breakfast-cup-sized flowers, huge, voluptuous blooms held up by strong bushes that can be 2m tall. The flowers are short-lived but their brief flowering season is worth waiting for. The choice of poppy shades is spectacular. I particularly like scarlet *Papaver orientale* 'Beauty of Livermere', candy-pink and red *P. o.* 'Burning Heart', the unmatched greyed purple of *P. o.* 'Patty's Plum' and the hot watermelon shade of *P. o.* 'Watermelon', but these are the mere tip of the selection.

Flamboyant in flower, they become untidy plants as they fade, so plant them with later-flowering perennials or bushy annuals in front. Oriental poppies thrive in moist, rich soil where they bulk up quickly, but they're also very tolerant of summer heat and drought as they retreat into dormancy soon after flowering when the mercury is rising. They don't divide well but are very easy to propagate from root cuttings which seem almost to hit the ground sprouting.

Perovskia spp.
Russian sage
Height: 1.5m

A swathe of perovskia creates a silvery haze of pale blue, stunning in the low autumn light of the northern hemisphere and equally serene on a breathless heat-filled day in the south. This is a lovely light plant, its fine, tall spires a wonderful foil for other bulkier, late-summer flowers such as dahlias; it's especially good in my border against the dark leaf and lavender flower of *Dahlia* 'Engelhardt's Matador'.

Perovskia will happily survive tough conditions if they have sun and good drainage. They are quite happy in rocky or arid spots and beachside positions. In cooler climates the plant will withstand cold winters and heavy frosts if cut back well before winter comes or leave it until spring.

Rosa spp.
Roses

Not all roses are resilient, but a good few are. Some varieties do well where it is hot and dry, others are bred to cope with a Scandinavian short summer, but many have survivor genes and can cope with a vast climate range.

For many years the only way for Australian gardeners to acquire an early hybrid or species rose was to take cuttings from old rose bushes abandoned in deserted cemeteries. Many had survived temperatures below zero and even regenerated themselves after bush fires, so it is self-evident that these roses had to be super-resilient. Among these great survivors were the Gallicas known to have been grown in classical times, the Damask roses renowned for their fragrance which are said to have arrived in Europe in the Crusaders' saddle bags and Moss roses, often mistaken for Centifolia, with a fuzzy, moss-like look to their stems. One of the most superb Moss roses is *Rosa* 'William Lobb', a huge plant whose double, deep purplish-crimson flowers fade to lilac-grey as they age, whilst another Moss rose R. 'Chapeau de Napoléon', approximately 1.2m high, has very fragrant, pink flowers emerging from wisps of small leaves that surround the calyx.

Roses that grow from their original rootstock are the most resilient. R. *roxburghii*, classified among the 'wild' roses, with its pink, almost white flowers bedecked with deep golden stamens, reappeared in a friend's garden within 12 months of its incineration in the bush fires that swept through west of Sydney. And R. *glauca* (R. *rubriflora*), grown for its greyish-mauve leaves, its hips and dusty red stems, flourishes in warm to cool climates. These are examples of just how hardy these old roses are on their own rootstock.

R. *spinosissima*, (R. *pimpinellifolia*) often referred to as the Scots (or Scotch) rose, is the bravest of the brave. It will grow beside streams, by the sea, in poor soils and in shade. Its form could be said to be open, with branches curving gracefully, giving an airy look – and it's very hardy. R. 'Stanwell Perpetual', a continuous-flowering rose with sweetly scented, pale pink flowers flushed with white, which grows in dappled all-day shade by my pond, is a sought-after R. *spinosissima* variety.

I have found the Alba roses to be totally adaptable, a reputation they have always carried, for it is believed they have the genes of the dog rose, the rose of the hedgerows, used for centuries as a reliable and impervious barrier. R. 'Königin von Dänemark' is an Alba rose I have planted everywhere. Never failing and ever healthy, this reliable rose, reaching over 1.5m in height, has large, soft pink, fragrant and quartered flowers that belong in the world of romance. R. 'Félicité Parmentier', another Alba rose, is recommended for the cold of North America, but will also successfully endure the heat of an Australian summer. The scented blooms are beautiful balls of pale pink petals fading to cream at the edges, flowering only once and backed by abundant grey-green leaves. This is not a large rose, reaching no more than 1.2m high, and it is eminently suitable for a hedge.

The Multiflora roses came to us from the Orient, plants known to be large and rambling, with two of my favourite roses amongst them. R. 'Veilchenblau' has sprays of tiny, single, magenta flowers flecked white and fading to grey, and R. 'Violette' is a rose that is covered with maroon, purple, lavender and grey, densely packed flowers of macchiato-expresso-coffee-cup-size that all flower together. Both are so hardy that this family of roses are in many American states regarded as noxious weeds.

But not all roses are so accepting and many have a decided preference as to where they want to live. In my Australian garden, the fashionable David Austin roses needed more water than was practical and only a few were accommodating. R. 'Constance Spry', with its large, cupped, pink, double blooms and spicy scent, and R. 'Graham Thomas', double, was a pure yellow, chalice bowl of flowers – both needed water, but they grew there as beautifully as they do in northern Europe.

From seeing the Tea rose, R. 'Lady Hillingdon', grow magnificently in my family's gardens, I thought it would suit any spot, so when I arrived at West Green House I promptly planted one against a wall. There it sulked for years, but at long last it has now grown, and magnificently so, after I gave it the shelter of another rose. I now know that it is a rose that needs a little shelter, even in southern England! Catalogues do say that, given this assistance, it is hardy on a south-facing wall, but I think it is a lot tougher although most walls will assist.

When I experienced my first very cold English winter I noticed that in the following season quite a number of the hybrid roses had regressed to their briar state. This happened because grafted bud unions are susceptible to freezing temperatures finding this to be particularly true of many of the standards and the grafted tree roses, all of which failed and had to be removed. Looking back, I have found that many of the roses bred by Kordes, Meilland and Leverhausen seem to have given a reliable performance, but the key to a resilient rose is its parentage.

Among the roses that have proved resilient for me in nurtured gardens (i.e. in good soil and watering when necessary) from the Mediterranean to cool temperate zones is R. 'Madame Grégoire Staechelin' (Modern, 1927), a vigorous, early-flowering climber with clusters of the richest pink flowers, 10cm across. I have American friends who tell me of it surviving temperatures as low as -23°C (-9°F) and for me it has endured periods of severe drought and intense heat where it has continued to look fresh and then flower magnificently the following season.

I grew R. x *odorata* 'Mutabilis', a China shrub rose that I first saw flowering in a garden outside Rome, in Australia in a very tough spot where it fared moderately well, which was surprising considering it was growing in a similar temperature. But here at West Green it truly flourishes with its small, single flowers having the sheen of Thai silk, changing from yellow-buff through pink to a coppery ruby. It can tolerate the extremes of the USA's climate down to -23°C (-9°F) even though English catalogues say it is suitable only for a warm space! However, I know from experience that it is happy in a wide climate range.

R. 'Cécile Brünner' is a Thumbelina rose, its

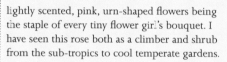

lightly scented, pink, urn-shaped flowers being the staple of every tiny flower girl's bouquet. I have seen this rose both as a climber and shrub from the sub-tropics to cool temperate gardens.

R. 'New Dawn', a vigorous, extremely hardy climbing rose with clusters of cupped, double, pale pearl-pink flowers, is tolerant. In the cooler UK garden I have placed it on a west-facing wall, in deep shade in the mornings, and it still flowers spectacularly.

R. 'Paul's Scarlet', a very free-flowering, old climbing rose with clusters of brilliant, unfading scarlet flowers is another favourite.

R. 'Bonica' is a vigorous yet exceptionally well-behaved spreading shrub with large sprays of slightly scented, fully double, rose-pink flowers repeating through into autumn. Hardy and disease-resistant, it flowers a little later in the early summer, continuing to bloom long after other roses have concluded their season.

R. 'Wedding Day'. Wherever I have lived I have planted this rampant rambler successfully. It produces flat, single, white flowers in clusters that emerge from amber-champagne buds,

maturing in midsummer. It is ultra-resilient and trouble-free.

R. 'Francis E. Lester' is a strong, healthy rambler with large, heavily scented bunches of small, single, white blooms, delicately edged with pink.

R. 'Madame Alfred Carrière' is a noisette climbing rose with fragrant goblets of creamy-white petals tinged with pink. A very strong, reliable and hardy old rose, flowering summer to autumn.

R. 'Jacques Cartier' (Portland Rose). This old Shrub rose, similar to 'Comte de Chambord' but with even more perfect flowers, is extremely hardy, tolerating poor soils, and temperatures as low as -29°C (-20°F) as well as heat. The blooms, which are repeat flowering, are a beautiful, rich pink rosette shape and are highly scented.

R. 'Blanc Double de Coubert', is a perfect, fragrant, white Rugosa rose that is doughty, having survived a flood, -35°C (-31°F) and rocky, dry soil.

R. 'The Fairy' is a miniature rose that grows little over 60cm, fanning out with tiny pompoms of lightly perfumed, pink flowers appearing in late spring and continuing until the first frosts! It is

a suitable choice for a pot, either to weep over an edge, or as a small standard centre-piece, surrounded by small lavenders and a toning trailing verbena.

R. 'Iceberg' is a Floribunda climbing, standard or bush rose that has suffered from over-popularity. However, it will put up with wind, cold and heat and still its sweet-smelling sprays of medium-sized, double, white flowers keep on blooming, although in humid conditions black spot does develop on the leaves.

There was a time when I felt that 'The Fairy' and 'Iceberg' were the two most over-used roses of all. This is easy to understand since they flower profusely and are tough and reliable.

R. 'Queen Elizabeth' is a Grandiflora, a cross between a Hybrid Tea and a Floribunda. What an extraordinary rose it is, glowing pink with large flowers like wine flutes just one flower on each strong stem backed by glossy leaves. It prevails with some care in dry heat but will endure up to 30°C (86°F). It likes full sun and compost every year, but is also durable in poorer soil. A large plant, reaching up to 3m, or as a majestic standard it deserves a place in any garden.

Phormium spp.
New Zealand flax
Height: to 2m

Captain Cook, on his great voyage to the South Seas, was amazed to discover how this plant was used by the Maoris for clothing, baskets, mats and for shelters. Nowadays it is a prized ornamental, with its wide-arching groups of hardy, sword-shaped leaves bred in a huge range of colours, topped by claw-shaped flowers reaching several metres above the foliage.

Phormium are indifferent to rough treatment – heat, drought, being trampled by children – but can grow monstrously big in rich soil in warmer climates unless confined. They subdivide easily when young, but I let one take over and serious machinery was needed to remove it. The colour range is exotic. Phormium 'Sundowner' has leaves of purple, pink and cream, P. 'Black Adder' is 2m of burgundy leaves and P. cookianum 'Tricolor' has green and cream leaves with red margins.

Santolina spp.
Cotton lavender
Height: 50cm

A third of one vegetable garden at West Green House has a grid of clipped santolina balls, spaced out as if on a parade ground. They are smart, dramatic and labour-saving, needing nothing except a twice-yearly clip.

Cotton lavenders have small, fine-feathered, evergreen leaves in silver, grey-green or brighter green. They have buttons of flowers in shades of yellow from palest lemon to bright buttercup, and a mounding, compact form. Santolina pinnata subsp. neapolitana 'Edward Bowles' is delightfully undemanding – just huge, rounded, grey balls of foliage covered all summer in lemon-yellow buttons. It also makes superb low hedges.

Along with the best Mediterranean herbs it withstands drought and months of sun, but it also survives long, dark winters as long as the soil is well-drained. Some gardeners like to cut off the flowers to keep the plant's shape neat or just clip off the dead flowers after flowering and tidy the plant up for the next season.

Scabiosa spp.
Scabious
Heigh: to 3m

Much loved by bees and butterflies, there are scabious to suit most gardens, from rather lax forms with small, dark red, mauve, cream and pink-shaded, pincushion-shaped flowers to sturdy-stemmed, wide-faced, blue and white varieties that seem to flower for months from midsummer on. The enormous giant scabious, Cephalaria gigantea, grows into a huge, spreading plant about 3m tall and wide and produces a mass of short-lived, pale yellow flowers in early summer, a back-of-the-border Goliath.

Scabious enjoy sunny, warm gardens and take a lack of water in their stride. Apart from the sturdy, bright blue- or white-flowered S. caucasica forms, they need stout companions or they're prone to flop. In hot gardens cut them back in late autumn after flowering; in a cool temperate garden wait until spring, or treat the smaller-flowered forms as annuals, with those that survive the winter a bonus.

S. 'Chile Black' has a deep maroon flower on 60cm stems and S. 'Chile Sauce' has a distinctly ruffled, purplish flower threaded through with white stitches.

Sedum spp.
Ice plant/stonecrop
Height: various

One of the most useful autumn perennials with heads of tightly packed flowers on stems rising from neatly spreading clumps of fleshy leaves. The number of sedum available seems to be multiplying annually, including new large cultivars for the back of the border and neat plants to edge beds. Some flowerheads are as large as cauliflowers, others small, ragged stars. Leaves can be bold, glossy purple, dusty grey, or pure green, some with white margins. Sedum are tough plants, that will flourish in almost any situation as long as they do get sun and are not waterlogged. Some forms with greyish or darker-coloured leaves can look rather dull in cool northern light before they flower, so they should be complemented by companions with good pale foliage, or perhaps planted against light stone, so choose a leaf colour to suit your situation.

Sedum 'Blade Runner' has red-pink flowers above very attractive, slim, toothed, green leaves and forms a generous 35cm-tall mat. S. 'Abbey Dore' is another compact but vigorous form with bluish foliage and a mass of deep pink flowers. The flowers of the ever-popular S. 'Autumn Joy' turn from pale pink to bronze-brown. Another

must-have is the ground-hugging, spreading S. 'Bertram Anderson', with copper-coloured leaves and bright pink flowers.

Sedum can be cut back at season's end or left until early spring. Their neat clumps of foliage and pale green immature flowers are often just as attractive as the plants in full bloom.

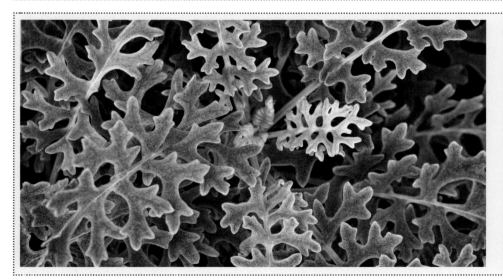

Senecio cineraria
Dusty miller
Height: various

My favourite time to view this plant is by moonlight, when its mounds of bright silver, ferny foliage look completely iridescent. Its yellow flowers are less interesting and these appear only in long, hot summers. Dusty miller does best in well-drained, poor soils in full sun, and it will tolerate frost but does tend to get rather leggy and woody in cold gardens where it is best treated as an annual as it grows very fast. Although this doesn't make it utterly resilient, it is one of the very best silver-foliage plants, so worth growing in any situation even if you do replant each year.

Verbena spp.
Vervain
Height: various

Leggy and good-looking, *Verbena bonariensis* is an inspirational plant in northern borders, but in warmer zones it can be a noxious weed. It is the ultimate 'see-through' plant, the stiff, ridged, almost leafless, dark green stems holding flat heads of clustered deep purple-mauve flowers from late summer through autumn, as attractive to bees and butterflies as to humans. In cooler zones it's best to establish plants in the greenhouse to place out after the frosts into a sunny spot and well-drained soil. I've tried overwintering them under a compost blanket to mixed success, so I'd really call them annuals in cooler areas, but where they are happy they will self-seed vigorously. Where *V. bonariensis* is tall and slim, *V. claret* is ground-hugging and spreading, the mulled-wine flowers rich above small, green-grey leaves and ideal trailing over pots or to soften the edges of late-summer beds in a sunny garden. It is frost-hardy in a sheltered position and well-drained soil.

V. rigida is a stunning, stiff, grey-green plant with vibrant purple-blue flowers that looks good in drifts under hot sun and in inhospitable places. Though very attractive, it doesn't tick the boxes as a resilient plant as it is not frost-hardy in cooler zones and dislikes overwatering, so must there be grown as an annual.

Viola odorata
Sweet violet
Height: 10cm

I am fast becoming a devoted fan of Pliny, who advocated placing a garland of violets around the head to dispel wine fumes and headaches – perhaps this was necessary after an afternoon on the violet wine the Romans made! On a more prosaic level, for years I was sure that the name of this plant in my childhood garden was 'Mrs Henderson'. Every time my mother and I passed an ever-expanding clump of this velvety, deep purple, scented violet, she would stop and point it out with delight, explaining that it was Mrs Henderson's gift. The delicate little flower may seem an unlikely candidate as a resilient plant but I know 'Mrs Henderson' continues to thrive in that garden in Australia where it has been subdivided for gifts many times, and good-sized patches of *Viola odorata* 'King of Violets' now inhabit my corner of Hampshire.

V. odorata produces intensely fragrant, tiny flowers in all shades of purple, mauve, pink, white and bicolours, rising from basal rosettes of deep green, heart-shaped leaves that run to create a mat of evergreen ground cover. Violets are woodland plants, spread by rhizomes in rich humous soil under dappled shade of overhanging trees. Adaptable and hardy to -15°C (5°F), they flower at the end of winter and will tolerate weeks of dry conditions in their ideal shady spot, when their leaves still manage to look fresh and green.

Allium spp.
Ornamental onion
Height: various

Planted in bold groups, some with heads almost the size of soccer balls balanced on ramrod-straight stems, alliums are the showpieces of the late-spring garden. So popular have they become that I'm convinced the mauve shades of May-flowering giant alliums have convinced Chelsea Flower Show commentators (held in that month) that all late-spring gardens are now mainly purple.

It's silly to generalise about alliums because these bulbs have such varied forms, from 1.5m-tall, purple giants to low-growing *A. karataviense*, 20cm high with starry pinkish flowers. *A.* 'Hair' is just an 80cm stem with wild green hair haphazardly sprouting resembling a bad hair day, *A. caeruleum* is about 60cm with small, cornflower-blue, spherical heads, *A. cowanii* has starbursts of delicate, white flowers at about 30cm.

Like those of the edible onion, allium leaves are less than ornamental, often browning and dying before the flower performs, so plant the superb large varieties through voluminous ground cover such as nepeta or euphorbia. They look best planted in bold groups, where the fading flowers can be left to dry *in situ*. Alliums are very accommodating in most soils and reasonably sunny situations as long as they don't get waterlogged and aren't too crowded.

Alstroemeria spp.
Peruvian lily
Height: to 1m

The Peruvian lily is a hybrid between species found in Brazil and Chile, with elegant, lily-like flowers in vibrant Inca shades of red, yellow, pink and apricot, often with striking stripes and blotches. Their exceptionally long flowering season makes the plants excellent value in the garden, and as cut flowers they will last in water for over two weeks. Abundant smallish flowers flutter from softly arched stems, and the best effect is to grow them to form large clumps. Eventually their stems bow over and sag, so companion planting is desirable. Mine have nepeta in front and push through rose bushes behind; I'm not sure this is the best solution but it is effective.

Hardy to -5°C (23°F), they start flowering early in summer and can be cut back after their first flush to prolong flowering into autumn. They subdivide easily and will withstand dry periods and ordinary garden soil, but flower most profusely on longer stems in well-mulched soil with reasonable water and full sun, though plants become lax and off-colour with too much watering.

Colchicum spp.
Naked ladies/autumn crocus
Height: to 15cm

They look delicate, but *Colchicum speciosum* are tough plants from the rugged terrain of western Mediterranean countries. Flowers open like large, purply-pink stars with white throats on leafless stems in autumn, giving them their old name of naked ladies. *C. speciosum* 'Album' bears goblet-like white flowers often tinged slightly green at the throat. Large leaves arrive after flowering and die back after their brief autumn performance.

I first grew colchicum in terracotta pots under bay trees where they must have baked, but they still multiplied and reappeared to flower each autumn as the season turned. They naturalise happily in grass in cool climates and will push through a carpet of fallen autumn leaves.

Crocus spp.
Autumn-flowering crocus
Height: to 15cm

Many crocus originate from the hard slopes and extreme climates of the Middle East, so are born resilient. *Crocus sativus* is the autumn-flowering saffron crocus with purple flowers and a violet centre around the orange stigmas from which saffron is produced – a spice we pay dearly for because it takes several thousand flowers to produce a mere 25g of saffron. *C. speciosus* 'Albus' is another showy autumn flower with white, star-like petals and a bright golden eye. Dormant in late winter, spring and summer, these super-tolerant bulbs will grow almost anywhere, naturalising in grass in the open and under trees in any well-drained ground where they will not be disturbed. The best gardener I know grows them under carpets of thyme; in another garden they peep out from under the hedges.

Crocus spp.
Spring-flowering crocus
Height: to 15cm

Heralds of spring, flowering for over a month, these are must-have bulbs in all but coastal areas. Among the huge range is *Crocus vernus* 'Joan of Arc', the largest pure-white crocus, and *C. vernus* 'Pickwick', goblets of white feathered and striped all over in deep mauve. Both have characteristic, prominent, bright orange stamens. They naturalise freely to bulk into huge drifts in a sunny lawn, grateful of any summer water but equally tolerant of dry years. Planted in autumn, they can be forgotten until they appear; as they fade; the grass takes over, so just strim or mow over them as their leaves die back. Crocus are completely easy-care, the only difficulty being that we are not the only creatures to find them irresistible. Just as possums in Mittagong waited for the tulips to be planted to dig them up and devour them, so the English squirrels believe that newly planted crocus are specially for them.

Dahlia spp.
Height: various

Not strictly bulbs but tubers, the first dahlias many of us were introduced to had showstopping dinner-plate-sized blooms, prized by their growers, they became supremely unfashionable for decades. Now it is a brave gardener who rejects them, for they are the bright lights of the autumn garden making outstanding statements planted in urns.

There must be a dahlia for everyone as they come in so many forms including spiky cactus, pompons, anemone-flowered, waterlily types, paeony and single-flowered. Heights vary from 30cm to 2m, and flowers from 5cm to 25cm across, with petals pointed, quilled, rounded or ragged. Their colour range covers almost anything you can wish for, many with splashes and stripes. The dark-leafed, truly hardy dahlias are deservedly popular, especially the 'Bishop' group in which small, single flowers glow above bronzed foliage.

Conventional wisdom tells us to plant dahlias as the soil starts to warm and lift them after the first winter frosts, shaking away the excess soil from the tubers and storing them in a box in a dry, frost-free space to overwinter. A rash of mild winters allowed many northern gardeners to keep the plants in the ground during winter, burying them under duvets of mulch, but recent severe winters caught many of us out and most of my own collection perished. So now I follow the rules: lift, store and pot on.

Of all the dahlia styles I like the flat faces, including *Dahlia* 'Ann Breckenfelder', a deep red and orange, its eye outlined in small petals of yellow. *D.* 'Moonfire' is another round flat face surrounded by dark foliage with petals just yellow, stained vermillion in the centre. *D.* 'Twyning's After Eight' has been hugely successful, its dark and bushy foliage supporting striking, white, single flowers.

Eremurus spp.
Foxtail lily
Height: 2–3m

Growing from crowns, like asparagus plants, rather than from bulbs, these dramatic members of the lily family hail from semi-desert conditions in Central Asia, so need good drainage, full sun and a cold winter. Given these three things, eremurus will grow anywhere, blooming like enormous starry wands that dominate the early-summer garden for a brief moment before exiting for another year.

In early summer their giant, waving spikes are briefly studded along the top 60cm with tiny flowers in shades of cream, pink, salmon, yellow and orange, opening from the bottom upwards. For me they have never been long-flowering, but whatever they give I'm grateful for. The flowering spike tends to bend and wave at the tip like a fox's tail, hence the name. They look most dramatic grown in large groups, their crowns planted at least 60cm apart on grit and in full sun.

The 2–4m-tall, deep pink spikes of *Eremurus* 'Robustus' make this plant look like a sunset from a distance. E. 'Romance' is 1.5m of salmon pink and flowers late, into July.

Galtonia viridiflora
Height: to 65cm

Looking as if it has escaped from the coolest woodland glade, this serene bulbous perennial defies the hottest or the coldest days, flowering in full sun or dappled shade. Galtonia has a strong, slender stem from which well-spaced, palest green, bell-shaped flowers fall in mid to late summer, backed by waxy, green, arching leaves. It is a seriously handsome plant that deserves to be more widely grown. It behaves perfectly in well-drained soil in full sun or lightly dappled shade, and needs no attention. Just cut stems back in autumn when flowers have finished.

Sternbergia lutea
Yellow autumn crocus/
lily of the field
Height: to 5cm

Despite the common name, this is not from the crocus family but a reliable early autumn flowering bulb happy in the driest spot or anywhere very well-drained. Its deep yellow goblet shaped blooms grow to 15cm. Once planted leave the bulbs undisturbed.

Muscari spp.
Height: to 15cm

Grape hyacinths are easy-to-grow, small bulbs that will in time colonise, becoming a sea of blue in spring. *Muscari armeniacum* is a traditional bulb we use for a naturalised planting, but there are all shades of blue to choose from. M. 'Blue Spike' is a plump and long-lasting, mid-blue double form, whilst porcelain blue describes M. 'Valerie Finnis'. Then there are whites: M. *botryoides* 'Album' is absolutely pure and M. *azureum* 'Album' green-tipped. Bicolours are very fetching: M. 'Mount Hood' has a topknot of white bells above blue and M. 'Golden Fragrance' is fragrant with newer-than-new colour, golden bells topped in purple.

Most grow to 15cm with different varieties flowering from March or April to May. At season's end, if they are growing in grass, simply cut them back with the lawn mower. They are excellent for pots, for once they have flowered they can be put aside and forgotten, surviving generally just with what rain comes. However do not do what I tried, planting in a very dry autumn a blue ribbon of 190m of grape hyacinth, for not one survived as the grey squirrels descended in their multitudes and commenced a banquet. At the other side of the world a possum can wreak the same havoc.

index

World Climate Map

- **Polar**
- **Temperate**
- **Arid**
- **Tropical**
- **Mediterranean**
- **Mountains**